THE
MEANING
OF
YOUR
DREAMS

THE
MEANING
OF
YOUR
DREAMS

By Franklin D. Martini

Ottenheimer Publishers, Inc.

Table of Contents

FOREWORD

This book was written by the late Franklin D. Martini. He was an astrologist, palmist, handwriting analyst, and interpreter of dreams who wrote many books.

Great were his followers who believed and followed Martini's every word—spoken and written. In his day, his name was a familiar one in the homes of those who were believers of the occult sciences.

There were many people who put great faith in dreams. They believed these nocturnal visions forewarned good and evil, happiness and sadness, good luck and bad.

For these people, Martini wrote *The Key to the Meaning of Your Dreams*. He listed the most common dreams and gave them his interpretation. We have modernized the vocabulary, without changing the interpretations, for the perusal and enjoyment of all.

The Publisher

A

"And the angel of God spoke to me in a dream, saying
'Jacob'; And I said, 'Here am I,'"

Genesis xxxi, II

Abscess

To dream that you are suffering with such an affliction,
denotes that your misfortunes are likely to overwhelm you.

Abdomen

To dream that you see this part of your body, foretells
that your greatest expectation will be realized, providing you
redouble your energies on your labors instead of toward
pleasure. Should you dream that this part of your body is
sunken or shriveled, foretells that you will be persecuted by
false friends.

To see your abdomen protruding, or swollen, signifies trials and tribulations, that may be conquered by determined
efforts on your part.

Abortion

For a woman to dream that she is undergoing this proce-
dure, is an indication that some scandal is hanging in her
immediate future. For a physician to dream that he is
involved in an abortion, foretells troubles to the dreamer
brought about through lack of attention to duties.

Abuse

To dream of abusing an individual, foretells bad luck in
your daily affairs. You are likely to lose money through the

influence of others who may induce you to act against your will. To dream that someone abuses you, foretells that you will be mistreated in your daily affairs.

Accident

To dream of such a misfortune, is a warning to avoid any form of travel, at least for the immediate time, because your life may be in danger.

Aches

To dream of such symptoms, foretells that you are too frank and open in your business dealings and others will profit by your ideas.

Acquaintance

To dream that you meet an acquaintance and the meeting results in a fuss or argument, denotes a division in your family, infidelity in love, or perhaps business losses.

Actor or Actress

To dream that you are in this profession, denotes that there is much hard work before you, but by persevering, your ambitions will be realized. For a woman to dream that she is to marry an actor, denotes that her ambitions will be thwarted. If a married man dreams that he is involved with an actress, it means family troubles. If the man is single, it represents friction with his sweetheart.

Adultery

To dream that you have perpetrated this act is, in most cases, a bad omen. Should the person you dream of be married, you can be sure that some trouble or misfortune is about to confront you. If a virgin dreams of adultery, it indicates an early invitation to a wedding. When a married woman dreams of adultery, it signifies that she will soon conceive, and is a strong sign that it will be a girl. If a single woman dreams of adultery, it denotes troubles and obstacles for her.

If a man dreams that he has had an opportunity to commit adultery and was unable to perpetrate the act through some physical inability, denotes a rival or competitor in business, sometimes an illness.

Affliction

To dream that you see a friend suffering with an injury or affliction, denotes the receipt of money or good news.

Afraid

To dream that you are afraid to go ahead with some project, tells of discontent in your household, and the prospect that business may suffer.

Agony

To feel agony as you dream, is not a good sign; it foretells of weariness and pleasure, the former likely to predominate. To dream that you are in agony over monetary affairs is a sign that you will hear of the illness of a close friend.

Air

To dream that you are inhaling hot air, is a sign that you will be influenced against your will. Cold air denotes a decline in business and, in turn, will bring family troubles.

Alligator

To dream that you see an alligator crawling, is a sign that you must exercise much care in any new step that you may be contemplating.

Alms House

To dream of this institution, is indicative that one's marriage will not be a solid one.

Amorous

To dream that you feel amorous, will lead you towards some scandal.

Angels

To dream of these heavenly messengers, relates to a changed condition in the near future; it tells of good news and a possible legacy not a great distance away.

Ants

To dream of these little pests, foretells of many trifling annoyances in your daily doings that will tire you without accomplishing much of anything.

Apes

To dream of apes, is an omen of sickness and disease. To see an ape in a tree, the dreamer is warned to be careful of false and deceitful friends.

Apparel

For a man to dream of women's apparel, denotes trouble, or temptations of some kind caused by a woman. If the apparel is flashy, illicit cohabitation may take place.

Apples

To dream of apples, is an excellent omen. To see apples on trees, tells of prosperity; to eat them, if they are good and ripe, is a signal for you to go ahead and carry out your plans.

Apron

To dream of an apron, foretells of an uneven course. For a woman to lose an apron, foretells censure and criticism from elders.

Arrows

To dream that others are shooting arrows into your body, denotes that a pending suspicion will be verified.

Ascend

To dream that you are ascending to some high point, but experience trouble in reaching it, foretells a disappointment.

Assassin

To dream that you receive a blow from an assassin, means you will be disappointed in your efforts; to see blood, caused by the assassin in any form, is a sign of enemies endeavoring to destroy your conditions.

Aunt

To dream of your aunt, is a sign that you will receive a reprimand for an action you are not guilty of.

Automobile

To dream that you are riding in an automobile, denotes that you will be restless and regret some deed or act that you have committed.

B

"I believe it to be true that dreams are the true interpreters of our inclinations; but there is art required to sort and understand them."

MONTAIGNE—*Essays*

Baby

To dream that you hear a baby crying, is a sign of disappointment and sickness. To dream of a bright, healthy baby, denotes success in love and many warm friends. To dream of a sickly baby, tells of many difficulties.

Bachelor

For a man to dream that he is enjoying bachelorhood to the fullest, is a warning for the dreamer to keep away from matrimony, for the present at least, because desperate, designing women want to marry him.

Bacon

To dream that you are eating bacon, is considered good; rancid bacon tells of worries and difficulties.

Baking

For a woman to dream of baking, is not a good sign; it speaks of illness and the care of a large family which may depend on her for support.

Bald

To dream that you see a man with a bald head, tells that

enemies are trying to injure you in your interests, but by persevering you will outwit their efforts and be justly rewarded.

Balloon

To dream of seeing a balloon, is a sign of a potential slump in business. To go up in a balloon means an unpleasant trip is in the offing.

Banana

To dream of a banana, denotes that you are likely to marry someone of very poor character and you will be unhappy. To dream of eating bananas, tells of friction in business. To see overripe or rotten bananas, tells of an undertaking which will be distasteful to you.

Banjo

To dream of this instrument, foretells a merry time for you in the near future. To see another playing a banjo, tells of slight worries which will soon fade away.

Bank

To see a bank without officers in your dream, is an omen of business losses. To see the tellers pay out money, tells of some careless act on your part.

Bar

To dream that you are behind a bar and mixing drinks, denotes a desire to cover your action by deceptive plans.

Barber

To dream of a barber, denotes that success and happiness will come to you after enduring much hard work. For a woman to dream of a barber, is a sign that her fortune will come very slowly and that patience is needed.

Baseball

To dream of baseball, tells that you will cultivate contentment and become a cheerful companion. To dream that you are playing baseball, tells that you will enjoy much pleasure in the near future.

Bathing

To dream that you are bathing in clear water, is a sign of good fortune; to bathe in warm water, is generally a sign of some trouble; to go bathing with others, is an omen that you must be careful in the selection of your companions. To see people bathing in such perfectly clear water that you can see the actions of their bodies, relates to honor and distinction. To dream that you are bathing yourself, foretells that you will offer a kindness to some person who will be thankful.

Bats

It is a bad omen to dream of bats; it foretells troubles, sickness, and even death.

Beans

To dream of beans is not good. To see them grow is a sign of illness. Dried beans means disappointment in material things. To eat beans, signifies bad news from loved ones.

Bear

To dream of this animal, is a sign of great competition in pursuits of every description. To dream that you kill a bear, is a sign that you will be able to overcome your difficulties.

Beauty

To dream of beauty, is an excellent omen. To dream of a beautiful woman symbolizes peace, harmony, and success in business as well as in love.

Bed

To dream that a bed is clean and neat, tells of worries ending. To dream that you are in a strange bed, is a sign of unexpected friends who will visit you soon.

Beef

To dream of beef that is raw, is an omen that bodily pain or an injury may be in store for you; therefore, it is advisable to use good common sense before proceeding. To eat beef that is pleasing to the taste, means gains in business.

Beer

To drink beer, means disappointment. To see others drink, means someone will reveal your dishonest scheme.

Bees

To dream of these busy little creatures, foretells a profitable undertaking. It would be well for the dreamer to act at once to take advantage of opportunity.

Beetles

To see them crawling over you, denotes poor luck. To kill them, is a good omen.

Beggar

To dream of a beggar, is a sign of poor business, generally caused by poor management. To give to a beggar, tells that you will soon be satisfied with your surroundings and will live in peace and contentment.

Belt

To dream that there is a belt around you, is a sign that you will meet a stranger who will create a good deal of gossip about you.

Bet

To dream that you are betting on games of chances, is a sign to be cautious in new undertakings. Unscrupulous competitors are trying to divert your attention into an illegitimate direction. Further, it is a sign that others are trying to wring money from you by some cunning device.

Bible

To dream of the holy book, denotes that some innocent act will be turned into unexpected happiness.

Birds

It is a favorable omen to dream of birds. If their plumage is beautiful, a wealthy and happy partner will be yours. To see birds flying, denotes prosperity to the dreamer. To catch birds, is a good omen. To hear them speak, denotes a work assignment which requires much caution. To kill birds, tells of misfortune.

Birth (Premature)

For a woman to dream that she gives premature birth, denotes that the very next child will be bright and achieve excellent grades in school. If a childless woman dreams of a premature birth, she will achieve success in her ambitions.

Bite

To dream that something bites you, is a sign of much work ahead; also, some indirect losses are threatened.

Blanket

To dream of a soiled blanket, signifies treachery. If nice and clean, it signifies success and an illness averted through exercised caution.

Bleeding

To dream that you are bleeding, tells of misfortune or possible death and also the possibility of many things turning against you.

Blind

To dream of blind people, foretells that someone will ask you for financial aid. To dream you are afflicted with blindness, tells that a great change is to overtake you—probably from the height of success to the pit of poverty.

Blood

To dream that you see blood flowing from a wound, tells of physical ailment and much worry.

Blossoms

To see trees or things in blossom in your dream, is a sign of peace and success in the near future.

Blushing

To dream you are blushing, denotes that you will be troubled over false accusation. To see others blush, tells of some blunder that was caused by an embarrassing act of yours.

Bones

To dream of seeing a lot of bones, is a sign of bad influence around you.

Books

To dream of studying them, is a sign of honor and riches. To dream of old books, is a sign to keep away from evil. To dream of hunting for books, foretells trouble.

Boots

To dream of old boots, indicates an illness and displeasure. New boots denote luck in your dealings and a possible raise in salary for your labors.

Bottles

To dream of bottles that are filled with some transparent fluid, is an elegant omen; it tells of prosperity in business and conquest in love.

Box

To dream of opening a full box, tells of riches and delightful journeys. To dream of opening an empty box, tells of disappointment and hardship.

Bracelet

To dream that you are wearing a bracelet on your arm, possibly a gift from a sweetheart, indicates that you may make an early marriage.

Bread

To dream of seeing a lot of bread, is an omen of peace and plenty throughout life.

Brick

To dream of a brick, foretells unsettled business and troubles in love.

Bride

For a young woman to dream that she is a bride, is a sign of money by inheritance, which will greatly delight the individual. To dream that you kiss a bride, shows a reunion between lovers.

Bridge

To dream that you're crossing a dangerous bridge, even though you've been advised against doing so, and you cross over it without a problem, denotes good business, and that you will achieve success quickly. To dream of crossing a railroad bridge with a speeding train coming toward you, and you are forced to jump down and hang on under the bridge by your hands in order to save yourself, indicates success and rewarded efforts in business.

Brooms

To dream of brooms, is a good sign; it tells of rapid strides towards success.

Brothel

To dream that you frequent a brothel, indicates that your reputation is at stake through your material indulgences.

Brush

To dream of using a brush of any description, foretells that a mixed line of work will be assigned to you, yet you will find pleasure and reward in doing it.

Buffalo

To dream of buffalo, is a sign of launching an enterprise, in which you will persevere and gain large profits.

Bugs

To dream of seeing bugs of some kind crawling out of your toilet articles, denotes an imminent illness to the dreamer. To dream that you crush a bug of some kind with your fingers, signifies that you will get a letter from a blood relative, telling you of a financial emergency and requesting your aid financially. To dream that your head is literally covered with bugs and that they are inserting their heads into your scalp, denotes a disappointment pertaining to honor.

Building

To dream that you are building, signifies that you will shortly meet with honor and distinction. To dream that you see a large building, denotes that you will shortly meet a new acquaintance and will afterwards become intimate. To a lady, this dream means a new admirer.

Bull

To see one follow you, tells of trouble in business. To see one horning a person, means bad luck may overtake you.

Burglars

To dream that they are rifling your pockets, denotes that you will have enemies to contend with. To see your home or place of business ransacked by burglars, is a sign that your good name will be attacked. Here, your courage should defend you.

Burn

To dream that you are burning yourself, is a good sign; it denotes that your ambition will be achieved and you will enjoy good health.

Business

To dream that you are going into business, but are disappointed in the quality of merchandise you receive, denotes disappointment in a letter containing important news. To dream that you have been unable to find a suitable location for the business you intend to open, you return inventory already paid for, only to learn the shipment has been destroyed in transit, signifies a loss of personal property. To dream someone is trying to put you out of business, denotes you have been cheated in some purchase.

Butter

To dream that you are eating fresh butter, denotes that your plans will successfully be carried out and you will be richly rewarded. To eat rancid butter speaks of many struggles relating to manual labor.

Butterfly

To dream of a butterfly, is a sign of happiness, success and much popularity.

Buttons

For a young woman to dream that she is sewing on buttons, denotes that she is to meet a wealthy man soon who will become her partner in marriage. To a youth, it signifies honor and wealth.

C

"And yet as angels in some brighter dreams
Call it the soul when man doth sleep.
So some strange thoughts transcend our wonted dreams
And into glory peep."

VAUGHN—*Ascension Hymn*

Cabbage

To dream of cabbage is, as a rule, not good. It indicates trouble in many forms. Should you see green cabbage it would mean troubles in love, and unfaithfulness in marriage. To dream that you gather cabbage, denotes that your extravagance might bring you poverty.

Cage

To dream of a cage with a bird inside, implies that much wealth and many splendid things are coming your way. It is also a sign of a wealthy marriage. To dream of a cage that has animals inside, if the animals appear tame and peaceful, means you will triumph over your enemies.

Cake Walk

To dream that you are dancing the cake walk, or performing cake walk movements, implies that you will receive news from an old friend regarding other acquaintances.

Cakes

To dream of cakes, is a favorable omen. A large and luscious looking cake denotes much success in some new enterprise. It also denotes that you will receive much pleasure from both society and from business.

Calves

To dream of a peaceful calf grazing on the hills, foretells of much joy and many pleasant associates, and a sign of early good fortune.

Camera

To dream of a camera, signifies that changes may bring about unpleasant results. To dream that you are taking pictures, denotes that something will occur which will be very displeasing to you.

Canary Birds

To dream of these singers, indicates unexpected joy. To dream that you own a canary bird, foretells that you will acquire much honor and distinction.

Candles

To dream that you see candles burn, denotes that a nice little fortune will be yours some day. To a woman, it tells that a splendid offer of marriage is approaching her, which she should not hesitate to accept.

Candy

To dream that you are eating candy and it is pleasing to your taste, denotes that you will have some money refunded that has already been paid.

Cane

To dream that you see a field of cane, is a good sign. It

foretells advancement in your business in the near future and is a strong indication that prosperity lies ahead.

Canoe

To dream that you are canoeing on a perfectly calm stream, tells that you believe in your abilities and are a born leader; consequently you should seek a venture on your own. To dream that you are on rough water, means much trouble in the beginning of any business venture.

Cap

To dream of seeing a cap, always relates to some public work, perhaps to take part in some festivity. To dream of losing a cap, means that your courage will fail you in time of danger and that you should be cautious.

Carpenter

To dream that you see carpenters at their work, denotes success for you, acquired in a legitimate way, with little danger of losing your investment.

Carpet

To dream of a clean carpet, which is a pleasant color, denotes much wealth and many true friends. To dream that you are laying carpet, you will have cause to go on a pleasant journey; also a profitable one.

Cars

To dream of cars, always refers to journeys, and many changes. To dream that you have missed a ride by car and are upset over it, denotes that you will be prevented in promoting your business.

Carving

To dream that you are carving a roast or a fowl, is not an omen of great worldly success, as others may constantly hamper you in your efforts. To dream of carving meat of any kind, and if your present business is poor, it would be advisable to change or conceive new methods to improve your present condition.

Cash

To dream that you have an abundance of cash, but it is not yours, denotes that your friends think you are greedy and unfeeling. To dream that you spend borrowed money, tells that your motives will be discovered in your deceptive generosity and that others will be offended.

Casket

To dream that you see a casket and remove the lid, denotes that you will adorn the casket of a relative with flowers.

Castor Oil

To dream of this oil, denotes that you are accusing a friend based on the hearsay of another, which is unjust.

Caterpillar

To dream of a caterpillar, denotes a tendency of being placed into embarrassing situations, and little chance for progress. It also speaks of deceptive friends. You would do well in being cautious with whom you speak.

Cats

To dream that a vicious cat attacks you and you are unable to chase it away, foretells that you have desperate enemies who will blacken your reputation and cause the loss of property through fire, from which legal difficulties may arise. If you are able to scare the cat away, you will overcome great obstacles. To dream of a cat that appears tame and gentle, speaks of deceptive friends who may not injure or harm you bodily, but who annoy you by gossiping about you personally.

Celery

To dream of celery, is a favorable omen. It speaks of prosperity and power beyond your wildest hopes. To eat celery, means that unlimited love and affection will be showered upon you.

Cellar

To dream of a cellar, is often a sign of approaching illness. It is also a sign that you may lose confidence in your business associate, and thereby lose property. For a young woman to dream of a cellar, denotes an offer of marriage from a gambler.

Cemetery

To dream of a neatly arranged and well-maintained cemetery, denotes that you will enjoy prosperity. It is also a sign that you will regain property that you had figured as lost, or perhaps that you will hear of friends or relatives that you have mourned as dead.

Cesspool

To dream that a sink or cesspool is overflowing and its contents go in all directions, denotes that stormy elements may destroy personal property.

Chains

To dream of breaking a chain, denotes torment and difficulties; to see another bound in chains, means a loss of money or an unpleasant business engagement.

Chair

To dream of a chair, indicates that you will fail to keep some important obligation. To see another sitting in a chair, speaks of some bad news.

Cheated

To dream that someone has cheated you in a deal, denotes that you will meet deceitful people who will try to steal part of your fortune. For the young to dream of being cheated, tells of quarrels and troubles in love.

Cheese

To dream of eating cheese, speaks of sorrows and difficulties. To make cheese, denotes profit and gain.

Cherries

To dream of picking cherries out of season, denotes an annoyance from an enemy or former friend. To dream that you are eating a dried cherry and to find that the pit resembles the shape of a diamond, signifies that you will hear of a bitter disappointment.

Chestnuts

To dream that you find chestnuts and eat them, denotes success in love, or that you will meet with some pleasant experience with the opposite sex. To eat boiled chestnuts, implies that you will have success in business. To dream you prick your hands with the burr, shows that you will be deceived by someone pretending to be a friend.

Chickens

For you to dream of a brood of chickens, tells of many cares and petty worries, some of which will ultimately turn to your benefit. Young chickens are good to dream of if you are contemplating some venture.

Child

To dream of children, is a splendid omen. If a woman dreams of giving birth to a child, it denotes a legacy. If a young girl dreams of giving birth, she should exercise much care or she will lose her virtue. To dream that you see a child dropping from a boat into water, and then being rescued safely, means good news is on its way.

Children

To dream of seeing several children around the house, is good, and if the dreamer in reality has none, it means success and many blessings. To dream of seeing your child ill or dead, it is well for the dreamer to exercise much care and good judgment, as the child's welfare may be threatened. To dream of a dead child, implies that troubles are imminent. To dream of playing with children, denotes that much happiness is in store for you.

China

For a woman to dream of cleaning or arranging her treasured pieces of china, denotes that she will be domestic and home-loving in her views. This will help her to acquire many cherished possessions that she will truly value as she creates a loving home for her family.

Chocolate

To dream of drinking chocolate, denotes that you will prosper after you have conquered your little difficulties. To see chocolate, tells that you will provide considerably for those who are looking to you for support.

Christ

To dream of Christ, denotes contentment and that you are greatly loved by your fellowmen, highly esteemed, and you will gain much from the prestige and influence of others.

Christmas Tree

To dream of this tree, tells of good fortunes and many joyful occasions.

Church

To dream of entering one, denotes benevolence and honorable conduct. To pray in one, joy and consolation. Should you enter a church in gloom, you will soon attend a funeral.

Cider

To dream that you drink cider, denotes a dispute and that you are confiding in friends who are not worthy of sharing your confidences.

Cistern

To dream that you fall into one, denotes troubles, caused through the trespassing on the rights and pleasures of others.

City

To dream that you are in a strange city, or lost in a city, denotes that you will soon change your residence or move away from home.

Clairvoyant

To dream of being clairvoyant, speaks of a possibility of changing your present occupation, which may arouse much hostility with your new associates, thereby making it unpleasant for you. To dream of consulting one, implies friction in your family affairs.

Climb

To dream that you are climbing and reach the desired spot, denotes honor and distinction for you.

Clock

To dream of a clock, denotes trouble from a backbiter; to hear a clock strike, you will hear some bad news, perhaps that of an illness, or the death of a near friend.

Clothes

To dream of seeing old and soiled clothing, denotes that a conspiracy is under way to harm you. Be cautious when dealing with friendly strangers. For a woman to dream that her clothes are soiled or torn, there is danger of someone maligning her character. To dream of clean and new clothes, is an excellent omen. To dream that you have a very large wardrobe, in fact, so many clothes that you don't know what to do with them, is a sign that you may encounter financial hardships. Sometimes legal difficulties are threatened.

Clouds

To dream that a clouded canopy is hanging over the earth, implies bad luck due. Should clouds turn into rain, this denotes troubles caused from sickness. To dream that you see bright clouds, denotes that happiness will be yours.

Clown

To dream of seeing a clown performing, denotes annoyances from near associates.

Coach

To dream that you are driving a horse-drawn coach full of people, signifies that you will be surprised by meeting, or a visit from, a friend or relative.

Coals

To dream of seeing red-hot coals, denotes a change and many pleasures.

Cock Crowing

To dream that you hear a cock crowing in the early morning, is a good omen. For a single person, it foretells an early marriage, and all the comforts of home. To dream of seeing cocks fight, foretells disaster in your family affairs that may lead to separation.

Cocktail

To dream that you are drinking cocktails, denotes that you will have troubles with your friends through a fault of yours; perhaps through jealousy that you may arouse by not treating them equally.

Coffee

To dream that you are drinking coffee, if you are single, is a sign that you will have oppositions regarding marriage. If married, dreaming of coffee means possible family trouble that can be avoided by proper care.

Coffin

To dream of a coffin, is an unfavorable omen. It means unavoidable losses to a man in business. To dream of seeing your coffin, much unpleasantness from the opposite sex.

Coins

To dream of gold coins, indicates much success; consequently, you may be traveling extensively. To dream of silver coins is not so fortunate; they usually bring about strife and contention in the dreamer's life.

Comedy

For you to act in a comedy in your dreams, is a sign that you will waste time by indulging in short-lived pleasures.

Companion

To dream of seeing an old companion, may bring about anxieties and perhaps temporary illness.

Composing

To dream that you are engaged in composing, denotes that some hard-to-solve difficulties will arise.

Concubine

For a man to dream of being with his concubine, is an indication that he is in great danger of public disgrace; his dual life will be brought to light. For a woman to dream that she is a concubine, denotes that she has little self-respect and does not care about public opinion.

Cooking

To dream that you are cooking, implies that you will be asked to perform some pleasant duties. Friends will visit whom you thought had no regard for you.

Copying

To dream that you are copying, indicates an unsuccessful plan which you thought would succeed.

Corn

To dream of corn, is a good omen; it speaks of many pleasures and a successful career. To dream that you helped to gather a large heap of corn, is an indication that you will rejoice in the prosperity of some friend.

Corns

To dream that your corns are painful, denotes that enemies are trying to injure you. Should you dream that you succeeded in getting rid of your corns, indicates that you may inherit a legacy from some unknown source.

Corpse

To dream that you see a corpse lying in a coffin, foretells that you will receive sad news, perhaps the illness of a friend, usually the opposite sex. To dream of many corpses lying in state, yet nothing is distressing about them, is an omen of great success, in some cases, an apology from one who has deeply wronged you in the past.

Corset

To dream that you have much difficulty in removing your corset, indicates that you will have an argument with a friend upon the slightest cause.

Couch

To dream of lounging on a couch, denotes that you are laboring under a false impression regarding some happening. Think twice before you speak.

Counting

To dream of counting some object, is a good omen. It denotes financial stability and that you are perfectly able to meet your obligations. Should you dream of counting out an object, such as money, to another, it is a sign of losses. To count for yourself is good, to count out is bad.

Cows

To dream of cows, is a good omen, as it foretells of an abundance of food throughout life.

Crabs

To dream of seeing crabs crawl, denotes that you will be compelled to solve many complicated affairs. The dreamer, if single, may have rivals in love affairs.

Cream

To dream of cream in any form or quality, is an excellent omen. It denotes that you will be associated with riches and have a bright future before you.

Cricket

To dream that you hear the noise of a cricket, is an unpleasant indication of serious news, perhaps death.

Criminal

To dream that you see the escape of a criminal who has committed a crime, denotes that you will be annoyed by friends who desire your influence for their own personal gain. To dream of apprehending a criminal, foretells that you will come into the possession of secrets that may jeopardize your freedom.

Cripple

To see an unfortunate cripple in your dream, denotes that you will be asked for charity by an old associate. It would be safe for you to give a helping hand, because some day you will be rewarded for your kindness.

Cross

To dream of a cross, implies that there is immediate trouble ahead, so prepare for difficulties.

Crow

To see crows in your dream, indicates unpleasant news. To hear them caw, means others may influence you against your better judgment in some business proposition.

Crutches

To dream that you are compelled to use crutches, denotes that you are too dependent and lack self-reliance.

Crying

To dream that some near friend comes to you crying and is seemingly in deep trouble, denotes that you will learn of some loss, either by fire or water, in which you may not be interested financially, but from a sympathetic standpoint. To a working individual, this dream may denote a loss of position. To dream that you are crying, denotes that some happy affair will settle into gloom. To see others crying, implies that you will hear about the financial troubles of some near relative, which is pitiful.

Cut

To dream of a cut, denotes a possible illness, or that the reprehensible conduct of supposed friends may disturb your cheerfulness.

D

"Dreams in their development have breath,
And tears, and tortures, and the touch of joy,
They have a weight upon our working thought,
They take a weight from off our waking toils,
They do divide our being."

BYRON—*The Dream*

Dagger

To see a dagger in your dream, denotes enemies. If you succeed in getting it away from your attacker, you will conquer your enemies.

Dancing

To dream of dancing, signifies much pleasure and a possible inheritance.

Dandelion

To dream of dandelions, implies health, happiness and success in your future.

Darkness

To dream that it becomes dark while you are traveling, generally means lack of success in something you are about to attempt.

Death

To see someone dying in great pain, means that you will shed tears before the day is over, out of pure sympathy for someone who is suffering.

Debt

To dream that you have a debt, and are unable to meet your obligations, foretells worry in business or love.

Deer

To dream of this animal, is a good omen. To the unmarried, it speaks of deep and sincere friendship. To the married, much happiness. To kill a deer, means that you will be slandered by those jealous of you.

Dentist

To dream that you are having dental work done, is a sign that a supposed friend is not worthy of your confidence.

Desert

To dream that you are wandering through arid land, denotes loss of property and possible life.

Destruction

To dream that the tools of your trade are destroyed, means that you will lose business.

Detective

To dream that a detective has a charge against you, of which you are innocent, implies that success is drawing nearer to you each day. To dream that you are guilty, denotes that you will lose your reputation and that friends will turn against you.

Devil

To dream of the devil, is never a good omen; it speaks of bad influences working against you, deceitful friends, etc.

Diamonds

To dream that you are wearing diamonds, is a sign that you will be deceived in love, or that your lover is unfaithful. For a man to dream of this precious stone, or that he is dealing in them, is a sure sign that he will become rich and gain high position in life. To dream of diamonds, means good luck, unless you dream that you have stolen them.

Digging

To dream of digging into the earth, implies that you will never starve, but you will have to work very hard for what you obtain. Should you dream of finding some precious metal while digging, this means a favorable turn in your fortune. Should the ground slide back into the hole, or the hole become filled with water, this means that in spite of the most strenuous efforts, things will not come your way.

Disease

To dream that you have contracted venereal disease, denotes misinformation from an enemy who is trying to attack your reputation to a near friend. To dream of diseases in general, denotes luck and success.

Diving

To dream of diving into clear water, denotes a favorable ending to some unpleasant ordeal. If the water is muddy, things will go from bad to worse.

Divorce

To dream of divorce, is a sign that you are not happy with your companion and should try to study one another and avoid finding faults, or the marriage will fail.

Doctor

To dream of a doctor, is a good omen, denoting prosperity and good health, particularly if one visits socially, for you will then not have to spend your money for services rendered. To dream that you send for a doctor because you are ill, may indicate some friction in the family. To dream of surgery, but no blood is seen, denotes that you will be annoyed by some person who tries to blackmail you.

Dogs

To dream of a vicious dog, yet you succeed in keeping him away, implies that you will conquer your enemies. To dream that a dog is giving birth, means an irritating disappointment will work out to your advantage in the end. To dream of dogs is, as a rule, good; but, if the dog snarls or barks at you, it means quarrels relating to business and that jealous enemies want to destroy your reputation.

Doves

To dream of doves, denotes happiness and peace, and that harmony will reign supreme in your family. It is a sign that you will be blessed with happy and obedient children.

Drama

To dream that you witness a drama, relates to pleasant meetings with some distant friends. Should the drama fail to be interesting to you, it means that you will be forced to associate with unpleasant companions.

Dress

To dream that you find a woman's dress, or to dream that someone else is wearing apparel in your wardrobe, signifies troubles and irritations caused by a woman. The trouble will usually occur at a very delicate moment that proves to be very annoying.

Drinking

To dream that you're going into a public place for a drink and see acquaintances whom you invite to join you, if you are having a fun evening, means that you will make an investment or begin a new business. Should a relative refuse your invitation to join you for a drink, this means that you will meet an old acquaintance and have a long chat.

Driving

To dream that you are out driving with family or relatives, and you come across unpleasant roads, denotes a pending unfortunate occurrence. For a man to dream that he is driving with a woman, is a sure sign of disappointment. For a woman to dream she is driving with men, foretells a gain or success in business. To dream that the horse you're riding is exhausted, or that you come to a place you cannot cross, denotes bad news relating to business.

Drowning

To dream that you see another drowning, or that you are drowning yourself, denotes much good luck for the dreamer. To a lover, an early marriage. To a girl, it will be well for her to keep an eye on her sweetheart.

Ducks

To dream of these fowls, denotes a surprise by a friend, who may call and dine with you. To see them killed, speaks of enemies who may interfere with your activities. To see them flying, foretells a change in business for the better. To hunt them, means a possible difficulty with your employer.

Dust

To dream that you are covered with dust, is a sign that you may have some losses in business through the failure of others. This would hold particularly true if it should rain on you while you are covered with dust.

Dyeing

To dream that you are dyeing fabric, is a sign that some disaster is ahead which may delay progress in your efforts, at least for the time being.

"Is this a dream? O! if it be a dream.
Let me sleep on, and do not wake me yet."

LONGFELLOW—*Spanish Student*

Eagles

To dream that you see an eagle soaring above you, indicates high ambition, which you will have great difficulty in realizing; nevertheless, you will gain your desires by persevering. Should you dream of killing an eagle, it signifies that you will associate with people of high standing who will bring you an influential position and power in life. To dream that you ride on an eagle's back, foretells that you will make a long journey, very likely into a foreign country.

Earrings

To dream of earrings, is an omen that you will have encouraging and interesting work to do.

Eating

To dream that you are eating alone, is an indication of losses and depressed spirits. To eat with others or in company, denotes success, happy environments, and undertakings that will be profitable.

Eel

To dream of an eel and that you are able to hold onto it, is a good omen. To dream that one got away from you, denotes that your business may suffer. To see one in clear water, is also a symbol of good fortune.

Eggs

To dream that you find a nest of eggs, is an excellent sign; it foretells happiness and contentment; also, a sign of many healthy children; to the unmarried, a happy love affair. To dream of rotten eggs, speaks of troubles and losses. To dream of bird eggs and that you crawled up a tree after them, denotes that you will gain money unexpectedly.

Electricity

To dream of electricity denotes some immediate offer which will afford you much pleasure and success. Should you receive a shock, a danger may lie ahead. To see a live wire in your dream, denotes that deceitful enemies are trying to overthrow your plans.

Elephant

To dream that you see an elephant, is a happy omen; it tells of peace and plenty. To dream of many, means you will gain fame and fortune. To feed one, denotes a job change.

Elopement

To dream of such romance, is unfavorable. To married people, it shows they are holding a position they are unworthy of, and may have trouble in these positions. To unmarried ones, it tells of great trouble in love affairs.

Employment

To dream that you are seeking employment, is good; it denotes that you are very energetic and dynamic and that your services are appreciated. To dream that you have a job when you are unemployed, means that you may continue to be unemployed due to lack of business.

Enemies

To dream that you meet an enemy and you attempt to apologize for some wrong committed, but the enemy ignores the apology, foretells a business disappointment. To dream that you overcome your enemies, is a sign that you will succeed in your business and become rich. To conquer an enemy, is a happy omen.

Engine

To dream of an engine, foretells an unpleasant start of a trip, but turning out well after reaching your destination. To dream that you see an engine wrecked, would indicate losses.

Engraving

To dream that you are involved in engraving, but through lack of ability, cannot finish the job, foretells a disappointment in a friend, whom you are eagerly waiting to meet.

Entertainment

To dream that you are a guest at an entertainment, where there is pleasant music, denotes good news from friends that are away.

Escape

To dream that you escape from prison, or a cloistered life, implies that you will have rapid rises in the business world. To dream that you make an escape attempt, and are caught in the act, speaks of unpleasant notoriety about you.

Execution

To dream that you witness an execution, signifies that you will suffer some loss, due to others. Should you dream that you are to be executed, but someone will come to the rescue and save you, denotes that you will succeed in overcoming your enemies.

Excrement

To dream of excrement, denotes a change in your social surroundings.

Eyeglass

To dream of finding an eyeglass, indicates that you have friends, whom you do not care for, yet do not wish to offend by telling them so.

Eyes

To dream of seeing eyes staring at you with a hard and calculating expression, warns you to be cautious of enemies who are trying to injure you. For lovers to dream of eyes, denotes they will have rivals that may be victorious. To dream of losing an eye, is an indication of illness.

F

"There are more things in Heaven and Earth than are
dreamt of in your philosophy, Horatio."

SHAKESPEARE—*Hamlet*

Face

To dream that you see a face, is a happy omen, providing
it is pleasant and cheerful. A frowning face, or a distorted
face, would signify trouble.

Fainting

To dream that you are fainting, is a sign of possible illness; also, distressing news from distant persons. To dream
of seeing others faint is a sign of good news.

Fall

To dream that you are falling from a high place, and are
frightened, but receive no injuries, denotes that you will
overcome a present obstacle. To suffer injuries would signify
obstacles that would go from bad to worse.

Fame

To dream that you have acquired fame, implies that you
are following a mistaken ambition. To dream of famous people, denotes that you will rise to the epitome of fame.

Fan

To dream of using or seeing a fan, indicates that good
news is waiting for you. Dreaming of a fan is also an omen

of reviving an old friendship which may, in the end, prove to be very profitable and advantageous.

Fat

To dream that you are growing very fat, tells that you will soon change from your present place, which will be good. To see others, is also good.

Fatigue

To dream that you are fatigued, denotes a run down vitality, which can lead to illness. In business, things will diminish in power.

Fears

To dream that you feel nervous and fearful over some matter, means that your prospective plans may prove worthless. For the unmarried to dream of being frightened, denotes disappointment.

Feathers

To dream that you see feathers about you, is an omen that your ambition will be achieved and that you will rise to great heights. To dream of ornamental feathers, means that you will become popular.

Feces

To dream that you are discharging feces, denotes a disappointment in money matters.

Feet

To dream that your feet hurt you, is an indication of irritations and troubles.

Fever

To dream that you have a fever, denotes that you are too worried and are wearing down your nerves needlessly. Live in the present, not in the past. Don't spoil today by worrying about yesterday. To dream of others being sick, denotes that someone in the family may become ill.

Fight

For a businessman to dream he is involved in a fight, means that he will soon make a change that will prove successful; to a non-office worker, it predicts a raise in wages. To see others fighting, denotes carelessness in the spending of money and time. To dream that you defeat your assailant, implies that you will win honor and wealth in spite of opposition toward you.

Figuring

To dream that you are adding a large column of figures, or solving a difficult problem, denotes that the dreamer must be very cautious in the presentation of a business deal, because it may fail to influence the party concerned.

Fingers

To dream of fingers, generally speaks of a gain. For you to dream that they are cut or hurt, implies hard work throughout life. To dream that you have lost your fingers, is an omen of legal difficulties over money matters.

Fire

To dream that you see something on fire and succeed in extinguishing the blaze before it gains much headway, denotes that you will be surprised very unexpectedly. To dream of fire, is a happy sign, so long as you do not get burned. To dream that your place of business is destroyed, denotes that you will become very discouraged regarding your business, but some unforeseen good fortune will give you strength and renewed hope.

Fireworks

To dream of witnessing an impressive display of fireworks, is a happy sign that good health and enjoyment will soon be yours.

Fish

To dream of seeing fish swimming in clear water, is very good; it's an omen that you will be favored by rich and powerful persons.

Fishing

To dream of fishing in clear water, and can see the fish bite and are successful in catching them, denotes that the dreamer will discover something which may be used to his advantage, resulting in wealth. If you fail to catch any fish, your efforts to obtain wealth will be difficult.

Flag

To dream of your country's flag, relates to great success and victory. For the unmarried to dream of their flag, indicates admiration from a soldier.

Fleas

To dream of fleas indicates irritation from close associates, which may cause you to lose your temper.

Flies

To dream that you see an unlimited amount of flies about you, denotes that you are in danger of being threatened with an illness; also, that enemies are trying to destroy your efforts, causing you much difficulty.

Flood

To dream that you are in clear water which floods, rises, and recedes gently, denotes peace and plenty. To dream of muddy water which floods and destroys an enormous amount of property, denotes sickness, troubles and losses, and unhappiness in family affairs.

Flowers

To see many flowers in your dream, denotes pleasure and profit. For a young woman to dream of receiving flowers, is a sign that she will have many suitors. To dream of withered flowers, indicates a disappointment.

Flowers (Artificial)

To dream that you see someone making artificial flowers, or bouquets, signifies that you will be astonished at an exorbitant price charged by someone who usually performs a service for you.

Flying

To dream that you are flying, is a very good omen, providing you fly low. It indicates a promotion in the near future which will make you very happy. To the lover, it is a sign that your sweetheart is true to you. To fly over clear water, is an omen of great marital happiness.

Forest

To dream of being lost in a forest, signifies profit to the poor and loss to the rich.

Fortune-Teller

To dream that you are consulting a fortune-teller, implies that you are undecided regarding some important matter. It is wise to trust your instincts and your first impression.

Fountain

To dream of seeing a fountain in the sunlight, speaks of pleasant trips and numerous possessions.

Fox

To dream of a sly fox, is an indication of thieves annoying you; to fight with one, speaks of an enemy who is crafty and subtle. To dream of a tame fox, is good; it denotes that your affections will not be betrayed.

Friends

To dream of friends being well and prosperous, denotes that you may soon see them and have an enjoyable time.

Frogs

To dream of seeing frogs leap around, denotes that you will have many sincere friends as your associates. To dream of catching them, is often a sign of a rundown vitality.

Fruits

To dream of fruit out of season, denotes struggles and unpleasant things to contend with; in season, it is always good; if the fruit is ripe, it is an excellent sign of good fortune to come to the dreamer.

Funeral

To dream of the funeral of a relative or friend, indicates riches, happiness, legacies, and a brilliant marriage. To dream of the funeral of a stranger, denotes scandal and deep underhanded practices.

G

"There is some ill a-brewing toward my rest, for I
did dream of money bags to-night."

SHAKESPEARE—*Merchant of Venice*

Gallows

To dream of seeing someone executed on the gallows, implies that extreme caution must be taken to avoid pending danger. To dream that you are hanging yourself on the gallows, indicates that friends are trying to malign you.

Gambling

To dream that you are gambling and win a great amount of money, denotes a loss of friends. To lose money by gambling, denotes consolation and relief from problems.

Gas

To dream that you are overcome by gas, denotes that you will have an accident due to your own carelessness.

Geese

To dream that you see geese or hear their quacking, implies that you will soon rise above your present circumstances. If you see them swimming in clear water, it is an excellent omen.

Gems

To dream of valuable gems, denotes that a happy fate is before you, both in love and business.

Ghosts

To dream of a deceased's spirit, if dressed in white with a cheerful expression, denotes consolation and happiness; to see one with a revolting expression, means a member of the opposite sex will flatter you in attempt to win you over. For a ghost to speak to you, implies that you will be protected from those who want to hurt or harm you.

Gift

To dream that you have received a gift, is a splendid omen. It denotes that you have no difficulties in meeting your bills. It is also an excellent indication of genuine feelings in affairs of the heart. To send a gift, means that displeasure will come your way. For a man to dream that he receives a gift from an unmarried lady, tells of friendship; from a married lady, illicit proposals.

Girls

To dream of seeing a lot of girls, foretells encouraging prospects and many joys. For a man to dream that he is a girl, is a warning for him to examine his sexual desires.

Glass

To dream that you are looking into a glass or mirror, refers to trouble in your family. To dream that someone gives you a glass and you let it fall, denotes that you will have an argument with someone close to you.

Gloomy

To dream that you feel gloomy and discouraged, denotes that you will soon hear of very discouraging news.

Gloves

To dream that you are wearing gloves, denotes honor, pleasure, and prosperity. To dream that you lost your gloves, tells that you will shortly have an argument with a loved one. To dream of wearing an old pair of gloves of which you are ashamed, tells that you will be deceived and may thereby lose something of value.

Gold

To dream that you find gold, is an omen of honors and riches, to spend it, sorrow and disappointment. To dream of hiding gold, denotes that you will get even for something done to you. To dream that you have a gold mine, denotes that you will become greedy and money hungry.

Gossip

To dream that you have been gossiping about something you had no right to, denotes that you will worry about a problem. To dream that others have been gossiping about you, is good; it means that you will have a very pleasant surprise in store for you soon.

Grammar

To dream that you are studying a book of grammar, implies that you will soon make a wise investment which will prove very profitable.

Grapes

To dream that you see a cluster of grapes, besides eating some, is a good omen. If they were pleasing to the taste, many pleasures and successes are in store for you; if they are sour and unpleasant to the taste, it foretells sorrow and trouble. For a young girl to dream of eating grapes, is an omen that she will soon marry; to pick grapes only, denotes that you will meet a stranger.

Grave

To dream of a grave, is not a good omen. To look into an empty grave, indicates unpleasant news, generally relating to losses. To dream of digging a grave, denotes that others are trying to prevent your efforts. To see your own grave, also speaks of enemies that are trying to harm you.

Grease

To dream that you have grease on your body, or on your clothes, signifies that plans you believed to be profitable may amount to nothing.

Groceries

To dream that you have bought a lot of fresh groceries, is an excellent omen. It denotes peace and prosperity.

Guitar

For a man to dream that he hears soft strains from a guitar, denotes that seductive women will try to trap him into marriage. For a young woman to dream of hearing music from a guitar, means problems in her love life. To play on this instrument, indicates a happy family life.

Gulls

To dream of gulls, is an omen that your possessions will increase rapidly in value.

Gun

To dream of hearing the sound of a gun, denotes trouble in work. To dream of shooting a gun, implies a misfortune. To dream of this weapon, is always a bad omen, whether you see it, or use it.

Gypsy

To dream of this wandering tribe, denotes that your immediate future is full of uncertainties. For a woman to dream that a gypsy is reading her hand, is a sign of an early but unwise marriage. For a man to dream of consulting one, tells that he is in danger of losing some valuable belongings.

H

"We are such stuff as dreams are made on,
and our little life is rounded with a sleep."

SHAKESPEARE — *The Tempest*

Hail

To dream that you are caught in a hail storm, denotes poor success in your prospective venture. To watch hail falling, indicates trouble and sadness.

Hair

For a woman to dream that she has beautiful hair, and in reality has not, denotes carelessness of her personality; also, poor mental power through lack of development. For a man to dream that he is losing his hair, denotes that he may become poor through his overly generous habits. To dream that you have hair cut close to the head, denotes that your willful extravagance will cause you to regret it. For a man to dream of having hair as long as that of a woman, denotes weakness of character. To dream of a bald woman, denotes poverty and sickness. For an unmarried woman to dream that her hair is turning gray, foretells that she will find it difficult to decide which one of her lovers to choose as a husband.

Hand

To dream of having beautiful and well-groomed hands, denotes that you will rapidly rise in your career and reach distinction. To dream that they are ugly or malformed, speaks of disappointments and hard times. To see blood on your hands, denotes quarrels and friction in your family. To dream that your hands are tied, tells of troubles in business.

Handcuffs

To dream of having your wrists handcuffed, denotes that you will be greatly irritated by enemies. To succeed in releasing yourself from them, denotes that you will escape the plans designed for you by your enemies.

Harem

To dream that you are the keeper of a harem, implies that you are scattering your best efforts on base pleasures. For a woman to dream that she is an inmate of a harem, denotes that she may resort to illegal pleasures, or enjoy the attentions of married men.

Harlot

To dream of being in a harlot's company, denotes an overindulgence in pleasures that may end disastrously. To dream of marrying one, means many undeniable and unpleasant things to face the rest of your life.

Harvester

To see many of them at work, denotes prosperity; to see them at rest, poor success in the near future.

Hat

To dream of wearing a soiled hat, predicts damage and dishonor. To dream of wearing a new hat, denotes a change of home and business, which will turn out prosperously. To lose your hat, implies that you will be irritated and annoyed over some business affairs.

Hatchet

To dream of a hatchet, is a warning to expect danger or death. If it is broken or rusty, you will have troubles over disobedient people.

Hawk

To dream of a hawk, foretells that you are likely to be cheated by one in whom you had the utmost confidence. To succeed in shooting one, implies that by persevering you will overcome all obstacles. To shoot at a hawk and miss it, denotes that you have enemies who are trying to malign you and destroy your good reputation in the community.

Hay

To dream that you see hay, denotes that you will be invited to a party, and that you will also assist a distinguished person. To dream that you are hauling and putting hay into your barn, indicates a very substantial fortune, and that you will realize a large profit from some enterprise.

Head

To dream of seeing a head severed from the body, and fresh blood around it, speaks of very bitter disappointments. To dream of seeing yourself with more than one head, denotes a sudden change for the better in your occupation. To dream of the head of a savage beast, denotes that your desires run on a low plane, and are given greatly to material pleasures; in fact, ruled by the animal world.

Hearse

To dream of a hearse, implies that an illness may enter your home in the near future which, however, may not amount to much. It generally means the death of someone near, such as a close friend.

Heart

To dream that your heart is paining you, or that you feel a smothering sensation, denotes that some oversight or stupid mistake may be the cause of a loss.

Heaven

To dream that you are climbing heavenward, denotes that success may come too late in life to bring happiness. To dream that you are climbing to heaven on a ladder and reach it, denotes that you will rise to great power in your present career. To fail in the attempt to climb to heaven, signifies that you are likely to meet with many losses.

Hell

To dream of being in hell, denotes great temptation will confront you which will be hard to resist.

Hermit

To dream of a hermit, denotes great misery caused by unfaithful friends. To dream that you live the life of a hermit, implies that you are very reserved and self-centered, and hard to become acquainted with.

Hill

To dream that you are climbing a hill, and reach your objective point, denotes success in a new undertaking. To

56

dream that you are going down a hill, signifies that the new undertaking will not be successful.

Hissing

To dream that you hear others hissing at you, denotes that you will not be pleased at the actions of a newly-made acquaintance. To dream that you are hissing at another, denotes that you are not truthful to yourself.

Hogs

To dream of looking at the actions of fat hogs, foretells a change in business which will prove very profitable. Lean hogs, foretell trouble with employees and probable difficulties in business. To hear them squealing, refers to unpleasant news, sometimes death. To see a litter of them, denotes that there is a great deal of good luck in store for you.

Homesick

To dream of being homesick, implies that you will refuse excellent opportunities for traveling, for which you will be sorry afterwards.

Honey

To dream of seeing honey, is an omen of great wealth. To dream of eating honey, denotes happiness in love. To lovers, an early marriage.

Horse

To dream that you are trying to pass one and can't because you are afraid, signifies that you will forget, or lose a valuable, but will find it again. To dream that you are riding a horse, is a sign that you will rise a step higher in the world, but if you are thrown off, it refers to scandal and disgrace. To dream of exchanging horses, denotes that someone will deceive you in a bargain. Selling a horse foretells a loss; to buy one, signifies that you will make money by selling property. To dream that you clean a horse that is full of dirt, foretells a coming sickness. To dream of horses in general, is good. To dream of a wounded horse, tells of news of friends who are in trouble.

Horseshoe

To dream of seeing a horseshoe, is an omen of luck in business; to find a horseshoe, denotes that your interests will advance beyond your wildest expectations.

Hospital

To dream that you are a patient in a hospital, is a sign of impending disease. To dream that you visit a friend there, denotes that you will hear bad news.

Hotel

To dream of seeing a fine hotel, denotes riches and extensive travel. To dream of owning a hotel, denotes a good deal of success, but brought about by your own personal efforts.

House

To dream that you go through an empty house, signifies trouble. To dream of building a house, is an omen that you will make a wise change.

Hugging

To dream that you are hugging a person whom you

admire, implies that you will have troubles in your love affairs and probably in business. For married people to hug others, not their partners, indicates dishonor.

Hunting

To dream that you are hunting, denotes that you are struggling for the unattainable. To dream that you succeed in getting what you're hunting for, denotes that you will overcome your obstacles.

Hurricane

To dream that you hear the roar and frightful sounds of a hurricane, denotes that you will suffer hardships in trying to avoid business failure. To dream that you look at the havoc caused by a hurricane, you will avert some business trouble by sheer good luck, or perhaps through the good advice of some good friends.

Husband

To dream that your husband is in love with another woman, denotes that he will soon tire of his present surroundings and seek pleasures elsewhere. To dream that your husband is about to leave, and you don't know why, implies that there is bitterness between you, which has not yet surfaced. To dream that you are in love with another woman's husband, denotes that you are not happy, and are trying to change your present life.

Hydrophobia

To dream that you suffer from hydrophobia, denotes that enemies are trying to prevent your plans. To dream of seeing others suffer from the fear of water, implies that business conditions will be affected by a death. To dream that an animal in this condition bites you, is a sign that you will be betrayed by a friend in whom you had the utmost confidence.

I

"My eyes make pictures when they are shut."

COLERIDGE—*A Day Dream*

Ice

To dream of seeing ice float in clear water, denotes that jealous friends will try to interrupt your happiness, but will not succeed. To dream that you walk on ice, denotes that you will waste much time and money on temporary joys.

Icicles

To dream of seeing icicles on trees or on buildings, denotes that worry that has been distressing you, will soon vanish.

Idle

To dream that you are idle, means you will fail to accomplish what you have begun. To see your friends in idleness, denotes a request for charity.

Idolatry

To dream of worshipping an image, implies serious mental trouble and bad luck in business.

Imps

To dream of seeing imps, is a bad omen for those who are ill, or for elderly persons. It refers to serious changes and grave hurts or disappointments to come to the dreamer in future endeavors.

Indigestion

To dream of suffering with indigestion, forebodes gloomy surroundings and pessimistic thoughts.

Infants

To dream of an infant, is an excellent sign. It foretells happiness and joy, good luck and general success. Lovers who dream of an infant may be sure of a happy and successful marriage. To a man in business, it foretells a successful change in business. For an unmarried woman to dream that she has an infant, denotes she will be slandered for actions she is not guilty of.

Injury

To dream that you have met with an injury, denotes that your friends will be kind to you, and whatever is wrong will be corrected.

Ink

To dream that you are using ink is good, but to dream that you spill it, denotes prolonged irritations and many spiteful things being done through envy. To dream that you have ink somewhere on your clothing or on your body, denotes that you will cause suffering and offend someone.

Insane

To dream that you are insane, forebodes a sad ending to some newly conceived project; also, that you may have to deal with illness. To see others insane, indicates that your relatives or close friends may ask you for financial assistance, because they are in dire need of your help.

Intestines

To dream of rupturing or suffering in your intestines, denotes family arguments. To dream of seeing your own intestines, denotes that you will soon suffer from sickness, which will cause you to lose time from work and thereby loss of a paycheck.

Intoxication

To dream of being in this condition, denotes an increase of wealth and sound body. To dream that you become intoxicated by looking at liquor, is a bad sign. It shows that you are trying to cover your plans by deceptive actions, which may bring you into the police court.

Iron

To dream of being injured by an iron, denotes great confusion in your business. To dream that you touch a red-hot iron, implies that you will have many disappointments with present plans.

Itching

To dream that you itch all over your body, tells of troubles in business, usually caused by enemies that interfere. These troubles will influence you to act in ways that are not in your best interest.

Island

To dream that you are on an island all by yourself and the water is clear around you, signifies pleasant trips and profitable ventures. To dream of seeing others on an island, denotes a struggle to rid yourself of unpleasant associates.

J

"In Gideon the Lord appeared to Solomon
in a dream by night."

1st Kings iii, 5

Jail

To dream of seeing others in jail, denotes that you will be urged to grant a favor, which you will not be happy about. For you to dream that your sweetheart is in jail, denotes that you will be disappointed in his or her character, so use caution; look into the situation before you leap.

Jam

To dream that you are eating jam, and if pleasing to the taste, denotes long and pleasant trips. To dream that you are making it, indicates a happy home and many true friends.

Jaws

To see the jaws of some large monster in your dreams, indicates hurt feelings between you and friends. To dream that you are in the jaws of some large beast, indicates that your immediate future holds many complications. To dream that your own jaw is broken, implies that someone has told a vicious lie about you.

Jealousy

To dream that you are jealous of your sweetheart, or life partner, denotes that enemies are exerting influence over you to commit something dishonest. For a woman to dream that she is jealous of her husband, denotes that her actions at home will give her husband material to make her the object of ill-timed jokes in public.

Jelly

To dream of jelly, signifies sorrow and trouble and, sometimes, that the most hidden secrets shall be revealed.

Jewelry

To dream of anything in the jewelry line, omens that much pleasure and riches will be yours. To find a great deal of jewelry, predicts disappointment.

Jig

To dream of dancing a jig, omens that you are lighthearted and gay, and love your work. To see others dancing a jig, denotes that you are too easy and benevolent, and may give money which will not be used wisely.

Jolly

To dream that you are feeling jolly and gay, omens that you will have many friends that look up to you as a leader and entertainer, and will have many favors come your way.

Journey

To dream that you went on a pleasant trip, denotes much success and happiness in the near future. If the trip was spoiled by accident, unhappiness and loss of hope.

Jug

To dream of jugs that are full, denotes that you have many true friends, and that they look out for your interest. To dream of taking a drink from a jug, denotes health and strength, and that you generally look on the bright side of everything.

Jumping

To dream of jumping and to succeed in getting to where you want to get, indicates success; to fail in the attempt, will bring about bitter disappointment. To dream that you are jumping over a cliff, denotes a bad investment and troubles in love.

Jury

To dream that you are selected to serve on a jury, implies that you are highly esteemed by your employees, and may ultimately select one to become a partner.

K

"God came to Laban the Syrian, by night, in a dream, and said unto him, take heed that thou speak not Jacob, either good or bad."

Genesis xxxi, 24

Keg

To dream of a keg, denotes that your present difficulties are imaginary, and therefore, it is well not to spoil today by dwelling on what happened yesterday.

Kettle

To dream of kettles, denotes difficult work ahead of you. To see kettles that are boiling, indicates that your struggle will soon end.

Keys

To dream that you lose your keys, denotes things undreamed of will cross your path. To find keys, is a good omen; it speaks of domestic happiness.

Kid

To see one at play in your dreams, means that you will be careless in your morals or pleasures, thereby breaking a loved one's heart.

Killing

To dream that you see someone trying to kill another, without success, denotes that you will receive money. To dream that you kill another in self-defense, or kill an animal under similar conditions, denotes victory to the dreamer.

King

To dream that you see a king, denotes that you are struggling in the wrong direction. For you to dream that you meet a king, denotes forgiveness for your faults. To have a long conversation with one, implies a conspiracy undermining your efforts from those you trust.

Kiss

To dream of kissing the hand of anyone, speaks of friendship and good fortune. To see children kissing in your dream, indicates many happy events. To kiss your sweetheart in the dark, relates to dangers resulting from improper meetings. For you to dream of kissing a strange woman, speaks of loose morals and deceptive honesty. To dream of kissing illicitly, relates to pastimes that may end dangerously, by giving expression to sexual appetites. To dream that you are being kissed by someone you are trying to avoid, means a minor illness to the dreamer.

Kite

To dream that you are flying a kite, denotes extravagance, or poor judgment in the handling of money matters. Should you fail in making your kite fly, means sad disappointment. To see children fly kites, denotes happiness and success to the dreamer.

Knife

To dream of a knife, is not good; it refers to quarrels, losses and separation. To dream that you receive a blow from a knife, indicates injuries or violence. To dream that you stab another, denotes that you have a poor sense of right and wrong; you should improve this ability.

Knitting

For a woman to dream that she is knitting, is good; it implies happiness, peace, and many bright children.

L

Laboratory

To dream of being in a laboratory, denotes danger of sickness, or energies wasted on useless projects. To dream that you are experimenting with drugs, and succeed in discovering a new cure, means you will achieve great wealth in your chosen field.

Lace

To dream of lace, is good; to see your sweetheart wear it, indicates sincerity in love and that everything will end well. To dream that you buy lace, means that you will marry a wealthy partner; if married, you will become rich.

Ladder

To dream that you are climbing one, denotes good fortune; in fact, great success in business. To dream that you fall from one, denotes that your present plans will turn out poorly; many things will arise to discourage you. To climb down a ladder, means disappointed efforts and desires that are misdirected from the beginning.

Lake

To dream that you are alone on a muddy lake, denotes many trials and irritations are in store for you in the near future. Should water seep into the boat, but you succeed in scooping it out, you will eventually overcome your difficulties and come out a winner. To dream of sailing on a clear and calm lake with good friends, denotes happiness and success to come to you.

Lambs

To dream of seeing a herd of lambs merrily running about, is a happy sign; it denotes an increase in your possessions, and that many good things are awaiting you. To dream of seeing them killed, denotes that you must sacrifice pleasures and infatuations if you want to reach your desired goal. To dream of having a pet lamb, or that you carry one, denotes great happiness.

Lame

To dream of being lame or seeing someone you know lame, denotes scandal and dishonor for the lame person, due to laziness and lack of action.

Lamp

To dream of seeing a lamp burning, indicates that your fortune will increase and that you will enjoy domestic happiness. To dream that you drop a lamp, means that your plans and hopes are certain to be shattered. To dream of carrying one, denotes that you are independent, you prefer to carry out your own ideas, and you seldom take advice graciously.

Lantern

To dream of seeing a lantern at night in the distance, denotes receipt of money unexpectedly; if, suddenly, you can no longer see the lantern, then hopeful plans will take an unfavorable turn.

Laughing

To dream that you have been laughing exuberantly, means success and many happy associates. To hear children laugh, means joy and health to the dreamer. To hear grown people laugh, a speedy break in friendship.

Lawsuits

To dream of being involved in a lawsuit, tells of enemies who are trying to influence others against you.

Lazy

To dream of feeling lazy, denotes that a business venture will fail through lack of attention to details. To dream of seeing others lazy, implies that you will experience difficulty obtaining proper assistance in conducting your business.

Leather

To dream of seeing piles of leather, denotes good fortune and much happiness.

Leeches

To dream of leeches, implies that enemies will strive to interfere in your affairs. To dream that they are applied to your body denotes an illness either to yourself or in the family. To see them on others, denotes stress and worry to friends of yours.

Legs

To dream of a woman's legs, denotes that you will lose your dignity and act very silly over a dull, uninteresting member of the opposite sex. To dream that you have a wounded leg, implies a disappointment, possibly a loss. To dream that you have more than two legs, denotes that you are working on more projects simultaneously than you can manage successfully. To dream that you can't use your legs, relates to poverty.

Lemons

To dream of seeing lemons on trees, denotes that you are blaming someone wrongfully, who will prove to you that you are mistaken in your accusation. To eat them, denotes troubles and shattered hopes.

Lending

To dream that you are lending money, implies difficulties in meeting your obligations, or in paying your bills. To lend articles, denotes that you may encounter financial difficulties through overgenerosity. To refuse to lend, you will gain wealth and will be highly respected by your friends.

Leopard

To dream that a leopard attacks you, implies that while things look optimistic at present, you will probably experience great difficulties before you reach the end. To dream that you kill one, denotes that you will overcome your obstacles. To dream of escaping from one, denotes a present difficulty which will turn into joy.

Letters

To write them to your friends, or receive them from them, indicates good news, and that you are interested in polite literature, such as poetry and drama.

Liar

To dream of hearing others call you a liar, denotes humiliations through deceitful friends. For you to call another a liar, implies that you will regret a former action.

Lice

To dream of lice, tells of worry and distress. To dream of seeing them on your body, denotes that you will have many irritations and disagreeable obstacles to contend with. To dream of catching them, denotes illness.

Lightning

To dream of seeing lightning, foretells of a short period of prosperity. To see the lightning strike some object near you, you will be irritated by jealous people, who will gossip about you to your friends.

Lily

To dream of lilies, denotes grandeur, power, and ambition; to smell them out of season, egotistical ambition. To see lilies growing with their rich foliage, to the young, implies an early marriage.

Linen

To see it, or handle it in quantities, denotes an abundance of riches. To see others dressed in clothes of linen fabric, denotes happy news, relating to money matters.

Lion

To dream of a lion, denotes that you possess strength of character and great determination. To dream that you conquer a lion, denotes a victory over temptation. To dream of a cage of lions, denotes that your success depends largely on your own personal efforts. To dream of being frightened by a lion, is a warning to be very careful in order to avoid potential danger. To dream that you are defending others from a lion and succeed, foretells that you will definitely outsmart your enemies.

Lips

To dream of thick lips is a warning to fight against your low moral character. To dream of sweet natural lips, denotes harmony and an abundance of living necessities.

Liquor

To dream that you are drinking hard liquor, denotes that you will have many so-called friends hanging on to you for selfish purposes; also, women of a questionable character will try to win your affections.

Lizards

To dream of lizards, denotes unpleasant confrontations with enemies. To dream of killing one, signifies that you may regain your honor. To dream that one crawls up your clothes, means that you will learn of bad reports from friends whom you sincerely trusted.

Lobsters

To dream of lobsters, is a happy omen. To see them, foretells riches and abundance of wealth. To dream that you eat them, means you will be insulted due to your pushy, overfriendly behavior in a public place.

Locket

For an unmarried woman to dream that she receives a locket, denotes an early marriage and many happy children. For her to dream that she loses a locket, means great sadness is in store for her.

Locomotive

To dream of a locomotive, implies that you are restless and fond of travels, and if the locomotive is operating, your ambition will be realized. To see one demolished, warns of distress and many disappointments.

Looking Glass

To dream of a looking glass, is not a good omen. It generally brings about some undesirable news relating to your plans; often disagreements in the family circle.

Loom

To dream that you are weaving on a loom, signifies that your life's partner will be a thrifty one, and many happy things are to be expected.

Lord's Prayer

To dream of saying the Lord's Prayer, implies that your strongest vocation would be in the mental health field, and you should concentrate your efforts in pursuing this type of career where you could help others.

Losses

To dream that you are losing part of your clothing, denotes that you will host a large party, or perhaps deliver a speech in public, or attract attention in a similar way. To dream of a loss of some valuable item, such as a watch or ring, etc., implies that you will regain as much or more than your loss amounted to. To dream of the loss of money would be similarly significant.

Love

To dream that your love is not reciprocated, implies that you probably will feel gloomy over some conflicting deal, thus causing you to become very undecided, not knowing which way to go, or what to do. If it relates to business, listen to your first impulse; if it relates to marriage, think carefully, not impulsively. To dream that you love an animal, denotes happiness with what you possess, and are easily satisfied.

Lucky

To dream of being lucky, means your wishes will be realized and ambition achieved.

Luggage

To dream that you have lost your luggage, foretells troubles in speculations, and possible family dissension. To the young and unmarried, it means troubles in love.

M

"In thoughts from the vision of the night, when deep sleep falleth on men, fear came upon me, and trembling, which made all my bones to shake."

Job iv, 13-14

Macaroni

To dream of seeing macaroni in large quantities, denotes that you are inquisitive and will accumulate some money. To dream of eating it, as a rule, refers to small losses, usually, in the matter of money.

Mad Dog

To dream of mad dogs, denotes that you will be greatly annoyed by enemies, who will try their utmost to implicate you in some scandal. If you kill a dog that suffers with rabies, you may succeed in overcoming their efforts.

Madness

To dream that you suffer with mental illness, and that you are acting irrationally in public, implies that there is sickness ahead of you; you should avoid carelessness relating to catching cold. To see others suffering with mental illness, denotes fickle friends.

Magician

To dream of seeing a magician performing, means you will travel extensively and that you possess keen observation.

To dream of being a magician, denotes that you are extremely fond of the supernatural.

Magpie

To dream of this sister bird to the crow, indicates quarrels that will cause bitter feelings not easily forgiven. Further, the dreamer is cautioned to be very careful about behavior after such a dream.

Man

To dream of a man with a fine physique, tells of great satisfaction and joy brought about through rich possessions. To dream of a man with an angry expression, implies that you will face many disappointments and problems.

Manuscript

To dream that you are working on a manuscript and succeed in finishing it, denotes that your ambition will be reached; but to dream of an unfinished manuscript, denotes disappointments. To dream that you have a manuscript returned, foretells unpleasant criticism of your actions.

Map

To dream of studying a map, or looking up some location, implies that you may soon contemplate a change. To dream that you can't locate the place you are looking for, denotes a disappointment.

Marbles

To dream that you are playing marbles, denotes that something will occur shortly which will take you back to your childhood's happy days.

Mariner

To dream that you are a career mariner, denotes many pleasure trips for the dreamer, and many visits to foreign countries as well.

Marriage

To dream of planning a marriage, denotes that happy times are in the offing. To be married, unexpected dangers. To see a marriage, sickness, and depression. To marry an ugly person, death, or some serious disaster. A handsome person, joy, happiness and great advantages. To marry your own wife, great profit. To marry a virgin, honor without profit. To marry one's sister, serious complications. To marry a servant, means that others are trying to deceive you.

Martyr

To dream of suffering martyrdom in a good cause, foretells of honors and public testing of character.

Mason

To dream of a mason at his duties, means a promotion or elevation in your social circumstances and those with whom you associate will now be more agreeable than before. To dream of seeing a body of men belonging to the order of masons, dressed in full uniform, speaks that too many are depending upon you.

Matches

To dream of seeing matches, denotes that someone will bring you happiness and contentment. To strike a match, means that unexpected good news relating to your business affairs will be coming to you in the future.

Mattress

To dream of a mattress, denotes that you will be requested to perform new duties shortly. To dream of sleeping on one, denotes that your surroundings will cause you to consider many good ideas.

Meadow

To dream that you are in a meadow, indicates that you will accumulate valuable property, and that your married life will be one of joy.

Meals

To dream that you see a meal placed on a table, denotes that you will let little things in life interfere with the big things, and thereby waste precious time.

Measles

To dream of having measles, signifies worries and problems. To see others suffering with them, means that you will be requested to assist at a charitable function.

Meats

To dream of meat that is raw, implies that trouble and discouragement is ahead of you. To dream of cooked meat, denotes that you have a rival for the same thing you wish to attain. To see it decayed and rotted, is a sign of sickness and death to you or someone you know.

Medicine

To dream that you are taking medicine with difficulty, foretells of troubles and distress. If it tastes good, an ailment that you will soon outgrow.

Melon

To dream of melons, denotes that you are ridiculing your best friend, making your friend doubt you and your friendship. To dream of eating them, denotes that you judge too quickly; attitude is what will determine your life.

Menagerie

To dream of visiting such a place, denotes trouble. If you are single and jealous, it denotes that you will be miserable during your married life.

Mending

To dream of mending an old garment, denotes that you will never try to take advantage of any trust again. Since you are an honorable person, you will try to correct the mistakes you have made. To dream of fixing clean garments, you will make some gains in the way of a speculative nature.

Merry

To the unmarried dreamer, to dream of feeling merry and lighthearted, denotes that a distinguished foreigner wants an introduction to you to propose marriage. To the married dreamer, success and increases of wealth are coming soon.

Mice

To dream of being in a room with mice speaks of family troubles and friends who are insincere. It also denotes that business may take a change for the worse. To dream of letting the mice escape, implies that you will certainly outsmart your enemies. To dream of feeling a mouse in your clothing, denotes that your so-called friends are actually trying to cause trouble for you.

Midwife

To dream of a midwife, forebodes that an illness is threatening you, which will almost bring you to death's door. Extreme care should be exercised regarding your physical condition after a dream of this nature.

Milk

To dream that you are drinking milk, is a very good dream. It speaks of peace, plenty, and many pleasure trips. To dream of spilling milk, relates to slight unhappiness in the home, usually brought about by continually finding fault with one another.

Milking

To dream that you are milking, but experience difficulty in relieving the milk from the cow's udder, denotes that possessions are withheld from you, which you will gain by holding your own and not be persuaded to compromise. If the milk flows without the least effort on your part, good fortune will be forthcoming.

Mine

To dream that you are in a mine, and meet no difficulties in going about it, denotes prosperity. To dream that you are lost in one, danger of failure in business. To dream of owning one, denotes trouble instead of anticipated pleasure. To dream that you are working in a mine, implies that an enemy is trying to interfere with your plans.

Minister

To dream of a minister, foretells that your friends are true and hold you in high esteem. To hear one preach, implies that you will assume new duties that will be highly criticized by others.

Minuet

To dream of dancing the minuet, indicates success. To see it danced, denotes friends who are congenial and very sincere in their actions toward you.

Mirror

To dream that you are looking into a mirror, indicates many discouraging issues. To see others looking into a mirror, denotes that others will work their way into your confidence for their own selfish motives. To dream that you break one, means bad news bearing the death of a loved one.

Miser

To dream that you see a miser counting a stack of money, usually relates to an increase of money. To dream that you are miserly, speaks of unhappiness from those who have tremendous egos.

Molasses

To see molasses in your dream, relates to pleasant activities, and many happy surprises. To dream of eating it, denotes unhappiness in your love relationship, brought about by the actions of a rival.

Money

To dream that you receive money, denotes good business, prosperity. To dream that someone tells you that you will receive money, foretells disappointment in money that you expect. To dream of finding it, signifies worries, but ultimately the outcome will be profitable. To pay out money, possible losses. To lose it, unhappiness in family affairs. To count it, and find an insufficient amount, troubles in meeting payments. To steal money, you must guard your actions. To save money, means comfort and prosperity. To forge money, shame and blame. To dream of swallowing money, reverses in luck may make you greedy.

Monkey

To dream of a monkey, implies that deceptive business associates will flatter you to advance their own interests. For a young woman to dream of a monkey, denotes that her lover may think she is unfaithful, consequently, it would be advisable for her to insist on an early marriage. To dream of caressing a monkey, signifies that your confidence will be betrayed by someone whom you thought was trustworthy and reliable.

Moon

For a wife to dream of seeing the moon in brilliant clarity, tells of love and happiness; for a husband, a sudden increase in money matters. To see the new moon, an advantageous change in business.

Morgue

To dream that you are going through a morgue looking for someone you know, implies bad news, likely the death of a relative. To dream of finding many corpses there, is a sign that you will be faced with bitterness.

Mortgage

To dream of giving a mortgage, means financial troubles ahead of you, which will cause you many unhappy nights in trying to think your way out. To dream of holding a mortgage against another, denotes that you have covered the worst period in life relating to money matters.

Mosquito

To dream of killing mosquitoes, denotes that you will frustrate the plans laid by your enemies. To see them, or be annoyed by them, you will suffer a loss at the hands of those who are your enemies.

Mother

To hear your mother cry, means illness either to you or her. To dream of leaving her, relates to difficulties in trying to resolve your problems. To dream of her after a long absence, denotes reconciliation between you and relatives. To see her dead, troubles to you or to your business. To see her dead in reality and you dream of speaking to her, denotes happy tidings. To hear her call you, implies that you are not following the right business. To see her with face drawn and haggard, disappointment.

Mountain

To dream that you go along a high mountain and are compelled to turn back because you cannot cross a sharp precipice, foretells of troubles and annoyances. To dream that you ascend a mountain successfully, implies that you will rise to wealth and prominence. If you fail to reach the top, you may look for reverses. You must be more firm and determined and the future will be brighter.

Mourning

To dream that you are dressed in mourning, or see others so dressed, is a sign of an early wedding in your family, or a near relative, and you will be asked to help in making the necessary arrangements.

Mud

To dream that you see others covered with mud, signifies that you will meet a very boring person. To walk in mud, means that you will lose confidence in someone you trusted in the past. To dream of having mud on your clothes; others are gossiping about you.

Mule

To dream of a mule, denotes that you will be irritated by the mental stupidity of others. To ride one, you will be very worried in your daily activities. To be kicked by a mule, speaks of change and disturbance in love and marriage.

Murder

To dream of seeing a murder committed, means that you will have to face many immoral acts caused by others; also, that you may learn of the violent death of someone you know. To dream that you are committing murder, implies that you are doing something that will ultimately result in losing your reputation. To dream that you are being murdered, means that others are secretly trying to steal what rightfully belongs to you.

Music

To dream of soft music, means prosperity and great happiness. Loud, unpleasant music denotes friction in your home life which requires tact in order to cope with it.

Mystery

To dream that you are involved in some mysterious affair, denotes that you will be urged and pestered to do something by strangers that will result in many complications.

N

"And he dreamed yet another dream, told it to his brethren, and said, 'Behold, I have dreamed a dream more; and, behold, the sun and the moon and the eleven stars made obeisance to me.'"

Genesis xxxvii, 9

Nails (Finger Nails)

To dream that you have long nails, means great profit. To dream that they are cut very short, trouble, dishonor, losses, and family difficulties. To see them torn off, great unhappiness, illness, and losses in the family circle.

Nails (Of Iron)

To dream of rusty nails, forebodes illness and decline of business. To see a lot of nails, foretells of many exerting duties to perform.

Nakedness

To dream that you suddenly discover your nudity and are desperately trying to cover yourself, denotes humiliations resulting in overindulgence in sexual activities. It is a warning to control those desires. To see yourself nude, refers to unwise associates which may prove disastrous. For a man to dream he is running and suddenly loses his clothes, denotes trouble from a woman he dislikes who is trying to force her attentions on him, or by ruining his reputation to her female friends. To dream of seeing others nude, denotes that scheming persons are trying their utmost to influence you to join them in their corrupt plans.

Navel

To dream of your navel being painful or swollen, refers to unpleasant news relating to father or mother, danger of death according to the amount of pain experienced. If the dreamer has neither father nor mother, it relates to suffering and sorrows from loss of an inheritance.

Navy

To dream of anything relating to the navy, usually refers to long trips, victorious undertakings, and joyful recreations. To dream of a dilapidated navy, foretells of many struggles and untruthful friends.

Necklace

To dream of losing a necklace, means sorrows, due from early bereavement. For a woman to dream that she receives a necklace, implies many happy gifts from her husband; many joyful hours in the home.

Need

To dream that you are in need, indicates that you must be careful or you may make some unwise investment that will have a distressing end. To dream of seeing others in need, denotes that you will suffer unexpectedly through excessive charitableness.

Needle

To dream of using a needle, is generally an indication of quarrels, which will cause you self-pity because no one will sympathize with you. To find a needle, means useless worrying. To dream of threading a needle, forebodes that you will be annoyed by the problems and unhappiness of others.

Neighbors

To dream of seeing your neighbor, shows much time will be wasted in idle gossip. Should the neighbor appear sad and troubled, this denotes dissension that will be lasting and bitter, and neither you nor your neighbors will care to humble yourself to make up.

Nephew

To dream of seeing your nephew, foretells dangerous rivals in both affection and business. To experience difficulties with a nephew, implies that you will have great obstacles in adjusting to disagreeable surroundings.

Nest

To dream of finding one, or to see one that is empty, denotes a bankrupt business. To dream of finding a hen's nest, relates to domestic affairs, such as contentment; also, that you will be blessed with many happy and healthy children. To dream of a nest containing bad eggs, means a disappointment is in the offing.

Nettles

To dream of treading on nettles or being stung by them, denotes that you are restless and never satisfied with your position, always complaining of your luck. You must be more firm and determined and things will look brighter.

Newspaper

To dream that you are reading a newspaper, indicates deceit, lies, and that you will be accused of cheating in your activities, which will endanger your good reputation to a certain extent.

Night

To dream that you are walking at night, denotes that unexpected hardships may be in store for you in your immediate plans, but should you see the night vanish before you, your troubles will disappear and be resolved.

Nightmare

To have a nightmare while sleeping, means that disagreements and worries will confront you. For the unmarried, it means disappointments are in store.

Noise

To hear a peculiar noise in your dream, foretells unpleasant news. Should the noise succeed in awakening you, a change for the better can be looked for.

Nose

To dream of seeing your own nose, signifies that you have more friends than you think; you are admired for your character and sympathetic nature. Your love of nature is exceedingly strong.

Numbers

To dream of numbers and to be unable to remember them, denotes that business will cause you uneasiness due to its unsettled condition. To remember them, implies good fortune is in store for you in the future.

Nuns

For a woman to dream of a nun, means widowhood or perhaps a separation from her lover. For a man to dream of a nun, denotes that he is more concerned about material wealth than he is about his spiritual self.

Nurse

To dream of nursing a child, denotes an illness to some member of the family. To dream that you are a nurse, implies that you will occupy a position of responsibility and trust.

Nymph

To dream of nymphs bathing in clear water, denotes festive parties with good friends, enjoying many delicacies and dishes of specialty foods being served. To see them out of water, would denote a disappointment.

"Then thou scarest me with dreams, and terrifiest me through vision."

Job vii, 14

Oak

To dream of seeing a tall oak with many leaves, means riches and happiness and that you will live to a ripe old age. To see an oak tree full of acorns, speaks of an elevation in your status. For the lover to dream of oaks, refers to an early marriage to his betrothed.

Oath

To dream of taking an oath, is an invariable sign of complications and irritations in your immediate future.

Oatmeal

For you to dream of oatmeal, forebodes many happy conditions; to eat it, good health to enjoy your good fortune.

Obituary

To dream of reading a friend's obituary, implies that unpleasant news will soon reach you. To dream of writing one, many boring duties will be delegated to you.

Occultist

To dream of an occultist, denotes that you will be forced to acknowledge an error made and to apologize for it. To dream that you are studying or going to become an occultist, means that you will be rewarded in some way for the kindness you have shown to others.

Ocean

To see the ocean calm in your dream, is good. For the business man, it denotes splendid remuneration. For the young, it means they will fall in love. To dream of being on a stormy sea, refers to troubles in business and disagreements in the household. To watch a rough sea from shore, implies that enemies are talking disrespectfully about you.

Oculist

To dream of consulting an eye doctor, foretells that you dislike your occupation, and a change would be advisable.

Offense

To dream that your actions have offended the sensitive feelings of others, predicts many obstacles in your way before your ambition is achieved. To dream that others offend you, signifies that others are criticizing your actions unjustly, which will cause you to lose your temper.

Offering

To dream of making a generous donation for the benefit of Christianity, signifies a desire to return to religion. To make a small contribution, denotes that after you have tried to lead an honest life, you will return to your former corrupt way of living.

Officer

To dream that an officer enters your home or place of business to serve legal papers, denotes unpleasant and discouraging news from those from whom you expected to receive good news.

Offspring

To dream of your own, signifies happiness and strong parental love. To dream of seeing the offspring of animals, predicts energies that will bring about prosperity.

Oil

To dream of spilled oil, denotes irreparable losses. To see it on yourself, profit and gain. In large quantities, your excess in pleasure may cause you suffering.

Olives

To dream of olives, is a good omen. To eat them, means many true friends; to gather them, means many favorable results in business.

Omnibus

To dream of riding through the streets in an omnibus or bus, implies that your friends are doing things which you do not approve of, which ultimately may cause the loss of your friendship.

Onions

To dream of seeing many onions, relates that your success in life will bring about much envy and jealousy. To eat them, is good. It means overcoming obstacles.

Opera

To dream of seeing one, predicts many good friends, and through their influence, you will attain much that is good in

life. To appear in one, hatred and jealousy, due to your digni-
fied and independent ways.

Opium

To dream of this drug, predicts that others are trying to
injure you in your prospective plans, through devious methods of which you are unaware.

Opulence

To dream of imagined opulence, signifies lack of strength
of character, and no determination. The dreamer should cultivate application of ideas of effort, continuity, and power of
decision making.

Oranges

To dream of seeing oranges on trees, is an excellent
omen. It means happiness and prosperity. To eat them, generally refers to illness, or news of a convalescent. To dream of
buying them, implies that complications will grow into profit.

Orator

To dream of becoming enthused by an orator's elo-
quence, denotes that an appeal will be made to you for a contribution which you will thoroughly believe due to the sincerity in the tone of voice. For a woman to dream of being in
love with an orator, denotes that she is lazy, impressionable,
sentimental, and spoiled.

Orchard

To dream of passing through a fruit-bearing orchard predicts happiness and prosperity. To pass through a barren
orchard, indicates trouble gaining a coveted object in life. To

dream of gathering fruit, means that success will be achieved in your business and personal endeavors.

Orchestra

To dream of hearing an orchestra play, means that things will greatly pick up in the near future, and remain very encouraging thereafter. To dream of playing in one, your sweetheart or wife will bring happiness into your life.

Organ

To dream of playing an organ, predicts much happiness and a comfortable life; also, that your position in life is pre-destined. To hear an organ played with selections that appeal to the heart, lasting and devoted friendship. To hear doleful music, you will soon learn of events that will sadden you.

Ornaments

To dream of receiving an ornament, denotes a contemplated change that should be carried out. To give one, guard your extravagance. To lose an ornament, a loss of a friend, or something material.

Ostrich

To dream of this bird, denotes that you will gain possessions through your unrestrained kindliness and diplomacy, mingled with deceptiveness that you will ultimately have to deal with. To catch one, travels and interviews with famous people are in your future.

Oven

For a woman to see her oven overheated, denotes many distant friends, which ultimately may cause her to relocate. If a woman dreams that she is baking, slight disappointments in her life will lead to unhappiness and restlessness.

Owl

To dream of hearing sounds of an owl, is a sign that a grief will soon shatter the nerves of the dreamer. To see an owl, implies that enemies are watching for advantageous opportunities.

Ox

To dream of seeing a fat ox, predicts good times and happiness is near at hand; while dreaming of a lean ox, poor times and little reward for your efforts. To see them fight, an indication of an early quarrel.

Oysters

To dream of seeing them served on the table, denotes friendship. To eat them raw, is a splendid sign of excellent health and fine success.

P

"In bliss, in dream, in silent night.
There came to me with magic might,
With magic might my own sweet love,
Into my little room above."

HEINE— *Youthful Sorrows*

Page

To see a page in your dreams, denotes that your marriage will turn out to be socially unacceptable. You should make sure the prospective partner is worthy of you before taking the step. To dream that you are a page, implies that you will commit some petty theft which will cause you to regret it.

Pail

To see a lot of empty pails in your dream, predicts an unprosperous condition. To dream that you see a filled pail, or carry a filled pail, denotes that success will be achieved, with all the accompanying pleasures.

Pain

To dream that you suffer pain, forebodes unhappiness, and that you will regret some trivial affair not worth bothering about. To see others suffering, denotes that you are holding onto a mistaken ambition.

Paint

To dream that you are covered with paint, denotes that your pride will be hurt through unfair criticism of others. To dream of admiring beautiful paintings, means that friends whom you thought sincere don't think too much of you. To dream that you are painting yourself, implies energy and vitality wasted on an object that will bring you little or no reward. For a woman to paint a picture, predicts that the person she admires adores someone else and that she will suffer from an unrequited love.

Palace

To dream that you are in a palace and are delighted with its grandeur, denotes that you will attain public recognition during your lifetime. To see one only from the outside, foretells of stress, irritations, and jealous rivals that will cause you suffering.

Pallbearer

To dream that you act as a pallbearer, foretells humiliation by the constant accusations of enemies. To see a pallbearer, denotes you will make yourself disliked by expressing your opinions.

Palmistry

For a young woman to dream of palmistry denotes, that she has strong psychic force and has the power to predict good things for others. For a man to dream of palmistry, foretells that he has the power to encourage the disheartened to succeed. To dream of having your palms read, predicts that in reality, you have many friends, but openly they may condemn you. Should you dream of reading palms, or that you have read the palm of another, means riches and fame for you. To dream of reading a clergyman's hand, denotes that your strong point is in the mental realm, and can persuade a crowd better than an individual.

Pancake

To dream of making pancakes, foretells that your common-sense and thrifty qualities will lead you to good fortune. To eat them, implies that a new plan will end profitably.

Pantomime

To dream that you are performing, denotes slight unpleasantries that will be a stumbling block for a short period. To see others perform, some indiscrete friend will reveal your secret.

Paralysis

This is a bad dream in whatever form it may be brought about. It denotes money troubles, suffering, long illnesses, and bitter disappointments to the dreamer. To lovers, affection that turns cold and dies away.

Parasol

For a married person to dream of a parasol, predicts unhappiness that will ultimately bring about disaster. For the unmarried, a desire to flirt and fondness of admiration.

Parcel

To dream of receiving a parcel, implies a surprise from one whom you least expect. To lose one, means that an offer will fail to materialize.

Pardon

To dream that you are innocently jailed and seek pardon, foretells present troubles that will ultimately prove to your advantage. To dream that your punishment is just, obstacles will lie ahead for you to overcome.

Parents

Should your parents be dead in reality, and appear to you in a dream, this foretells troubles. You must exercise care in the planning of affairs. To dream of living parents, and see that they are happy and well, denotes fortunate changes.

Park

To dream of going through a beautiful park, predicts pleasant happenings to the dreamer. To a lover, the park will glide smoothly on the matrimonial sea.

Parrot

To dream of a parrot, means discovering a secret. For the unmarried to dream of owning a parrot, lovers' quarrels may be looked for.

Parting

To dream of a parting from friends that is emotional, implies that little things will annoy you greatly.

Partridge

To dream of this bird, foretells intimacy with ungrateful partners. To kill them, means that you have the power of acquiring but not accumulating wealth. To eat them, and if you enjoy the taste, enjoyment and success.

Paste

To dream of paste on your clothes, denotes that those with whom you are dealing, are hiding their bad habits in order to win your confidence and gain their selfish purpose through your influence. To dream that you are pasting, predicts that matters you thought were settled must be reviewed.

Pastry

To dream of making pastry, denotes pleasures and profit. To see it, denotes that some sly person is seeking to deceive you. To eat it, foretells many happy times among friends.

Patent

To dream that you have conceived a patent, denotes that the dreamer seeks, reasons, calculates, and wants positive proof before going ahead. To dream that you tried to conceive a patent and have failed, predicts that you reason things to death; you should trust your first impressions more.

Pauper

To dream that you are a pauper, refers to sudden and unexpected wealth. To dream of seeing other paupers, denotes you will be requested to offer assistance.

Pavement

To dream that you are walking on a pavement that caves in, but you are not hurt, denotes that a new business prospect which is an excellent opportunity will soon come your way.

Pawn Shop

To dream that you have pawned articles, denotes that family problems are staring you in the face which are your fault. To redeem a pawned article, indicates that many of your efforts were misdirected, but are now on the right track.

Peaches

To dream of eating peaches in season, indicates much satisfaction and enjoyment. To dream of them out of season, means struggles and disappointment.

Peacock

To dream of seeing one spreading his tail, means wealth and an indication of a very handsome partner. For a woman to dream that she owns a peacock, denotes that she is placing too much confidence in a certain person. Be careful of how much of your past you reveal. To dream of pulling his beautiful feathers, denotes that you will fail to obtain a certain object due to your proud spirit.

Pearls

To dream of pearls, is a favorable omen. It means excellent business and not much to annoy you. For a girl to dream of receiving a string of pearls from her lover, means many good things for her. For her to dream of breaking her pearls, would imply deep sadness through misunderstanding. To lose them, would mean about the same.

Pears

To dream of eating pears in season, foretells of happiness, particularly if they are sweet. To dream of green or decayed pears, sickness and disappointment lie ahead.

Peas

To dream of eating them, and if they are luscious to the taste, denotes an increase in business with quick profits. To dream of eating them raw would imply problems and disappointments that the dreamer would have to overcome.

Pelican

To see a pelican in your dream, relates to success slowly reached. To dream of catching one, you will divert an enemy before he does much damage to you.

Penalties

To dream that you are compelled to pay a penalty, refers to loss and sickness. To dream that you get off free, means honors and distinction. To dream that a penalty will be imposed on you, denotes that you will be mixed up in a misunderstanding, due to some argument.

Penitentiary

To dream of being a confined convict, denotes that you will have many petty things to annoy you. To escape from one, you will conquer those that are against you. To dream of a penitentiary, foretells that you will have disagreeable duties to perform.

People

To dream of a crowd of people at a fashionable affair, denotes many pleasant things to the dreamer. To dream of a boisterous crowd of people, predicts that conditions will prove very discouraging to you, perhaps brought about by family problems. To dream of seeing many well-behaved people, is always good, to see them otherwise, means trouble of some kind.

Pepper

To dream of pepper, is not good. It relates to worry, concern, irritation, and a meeting with someone who is difficult to get along with.

Perfume

To dream of perfuming yourself, denotes that you will hear many complimentary things said about you. To dream of receiving perfume as a gift, predicts many advantages and that you will associate with people of intelligence. To smell it, is always good.

Perspiration

To dream that you are perspiring freely, denotes that the problems troubling you will soon disappear, and you will prove to those who have been gossiping about you that you are not as bad as they thought.

Petticoat

For a young woman to dream that she is losing her petticoat in some public place, denotes that her lover is losing interest in her. The woman should be more reserved and not too obvious about how she feels in order to keep the man guessing, because the man loves to chase something which is difficult to attain. To dream of a petticoat with many contrasting colors, many petty annoyances are to be faced. To dream of a very rich and expensive petticoat, denotes pride and dignity.

Phantom

To dream that such a phantom is chasing you, but that you succeed in getting away, denotes joy and freedom from your present worries. To touch you, unpleasant experiences to the dreamer. To see one in black, troubles from a woman. To see one running away from you, troubles are at an end.

Pheasant

To dream of this bird, denotes great happiness. To kill one, denotes that you must fight against a certain temptation. To eat one, denotes that your high living and overeating will produce a weak digestive system.

Photograph

To dream that you are having your picture taken, denotes that you will be mistaken for someone else and will be very embarrassed. To see pictures, denotes happiness. To see yourself in an amusing pose, implies that gossips are talking about you. To dream that you are taking photographs, predicts that your love for the aesthetic is interfering with your daily business concerns.

Physician

For a girl to dream of a doctor, implies that she is foolishly thinking of things which may cause trouble for her. To dream that she is sick, and has the doctor, denotes that sorrow is in store for her. For a married woman to dream of a physician, denotes that she lacks self-control and imagines illness which does not exist.

Piano

To dream of hearing pleasing piano music, denotes joy and contentment. Loud, harsh music, possible family disagreements. For an unmarried woman to dream that she is playing a difficult piece of music, predicts a success in love with a disinterested lover.

Pickles

To dream of pickles, means misdirected efforts and energy wasted, not liking your present job, but performing your duties just to remain employed or only for a paycheck. To dream of pickles also tells of troubles in love, but not necessarily separation. For a girl to dream of eating pickles, denotes many rivals for the person she loves.

Pickpocket

To see a pickpocket in your dream, foretells that an enemy will annoy you very much and cause others to misjudge. To dream of having your own pockets picked, denotes that a friend will become an enemy through the spiteful actions of others.

Picnic

To dream that you help to make a picnic a huge success, implies an advancement and ultimate fun and success. To dream that your planned activities at a picnic are interrupted for some reason, means that your plans will not be completed quite as you would have liked.

Pictures

To dream that you are drawing pictures, denotes a lot of hard work with very little profit. To see them, means that surprises from unexpected friends are in store for you in the future.

Pies

For an unmarried woman to dream of baking a pie, signifies that her love for admiration and desire to flirt may lead into trouble. To dream of eating pies, enemies are talking disrespectfully about you.

Pig

To dream of fat, healthy pigs, denotes that your energies will be rewarded. To dream of lean, sickly looking pigs, means a great deal of hard work and efforts that will ultimately prove to be useless.

Pillow

For a woman to dream that she is making a pillow, denotes a comfortable, peaceful life and that she will be surrounded by luxuries. To dream of many beautiful pillows, predicts a love for romance and sentiment.

Pimples

To dream of having pimples on your body, means great wealth, both in real estate and personal property. To see them on others, is an indication of disgust, due to the gossip that is being repeated by others.

Pins

To dream that you do not allow someone to prick you with a pin, denotes a surprise. For example, you will receive a great deal more than you originally asked for, or expected. To dream of swallowing a pin, denotes that unforeseen circumstances will result in an unpleasant situation.

Pipe

To dream that you follow a loved one by crawling through a long, dark, rusty sewer pipe and experience a smothered feeling, denotes a bitter disappointment. To dream of smoking a pipe, means that you will meet an old acquaintance whom you thought was angry with you. To see a lot of old broken iron pipes, poor business.

Pistol

To dream of shooting a pistol, denotes that you will apologize to someone for a false accusation you made based solely on something you heard. To dream of these pistols in general, foretells difficulties.

Pitcher

To dream of a pitcher, denotes a loss, generally due to your own carelessness, sometimes due to others. To dream of a broken pitcher, refers to the loss of friends.

Plague

To dream of a place where a plague is rampant, implies poor business terminating in thorough discouragement. Even the home may be shattered due to poor business. To dream that you are afflicted with it, denotes that you will become confused mentally over conditions. This is a warning that you must not lose self-control.

Plane

To dream you are on a plane, denotes that your efforts will be rewarded and your ambition achieved. To see others working on a plane, foretells good business conditions.

Plank

To dream of walking across a plank safely, denotes that a project will be successful. To dream of crossing a rotten plank and having it break, means unhappiness lies ahead.

Play

To dream of attending a play, is a sign of short-lived pleasures. For the unmarried to dream of a play, denotes that their sweethearts will act indifferently, causing them to suspect loss of interest in them.

Plow

To dream of seeing people plowing, denotes good fortune and affirms that you are on the road to success. If you dream that you are doing the plowing, splendid rewards for your ongoing efforts will come soon.

Pocketbook

To dream that you find a pocketbook filled with money, is an excellent omen for your immediate success. To find one that is empty, denotes shattered hopes.

Poison

To dream of seeing others poisoned, denotes an illness generally brought about through a contagious disease. To dream that you are poisoned, foretells news from a distance that is painful and disturbing to you. To dream that you are preparing to poison someone, denotes many plans you believed would work will prove unsuccessful.

Police

To dream that the police want to arrest you for a charge you know nothing about, denotes that you will win a competition relating to business conditions. To feel that you are guilty of a charge, denotes the conclusion of bad business.

Polishing

To dream that you are polishing articles that are rusty and ugly, and succeed in improving their appearance, implies that you will rise to great heights of power. If your efforts are without results, struggles and disappointment lie ahead.

Poorhouse

To dream of entering a poorhouse, denotes that you have deceptive friends who, in reality, only need you to further their own selfish ambitions in their efforts to be successful. Re-examine your friendships carefully.

Porcupines

To dream of seeing a porcupine, foretells disagreements relating to business. For the unmarried to dream of a porcupine, predicts a delicate affair relating to a sweetheart.

Portrait

To dream of admiring a beautiful portrait of someone you know, denotes long life to that individual. To give, or receive a portrait, predicts that you will hear deceptive flattery from an associate with whom you work closely.

Potatoes

To dream of potatoes in general, is a good omen. To dream that you are planting potatoes, denotes that your ambitions will be achieved. To dig them, an excellent omen for success. To eat them, you will achieve success.

Poultry

To dream of live poultry, denotes valuable time wasted on silly pleasures. To dream of stuffed poultry, predicts that your generous ways will bring you many friends who will stick by you while your money lasts.

Prairie

To see a prairie in your dream, denotes luxuries and a trouble-free life; also, that you are very popular. To dream that you are lost on one, indicates that you may experience sadness and disappointments.

Prayer

To dream of saying your prayers, denotes disagreements and trouble among friends. To dream of seeing others saying their prayers, predicts happy events.

Preacher

To dream that you are a preacher, or are preaching, signifies that plans will fail to materialize. To dream of hearing a preacher preach, signifies dissatisfaction caused by others who are blaming you for something.

Precipice

To dream of falling over a precipice, denotes hostility, anger, and danger for the dreamer. To dream of being on the edge of a precipice, relates to impending losses and disasters.

Pregnancy

For a husband to dream that his wife is pregnant, and in reality, she is pregnant, denotes a safe delivery, with no complications. For a woman to dream that she is pregnant, implies that disagreements and misunderstanding will be her chief obstacle in life. For a virgin, or unmarried woman to dream of being pregnant, is a warning that she is considering a marriage that may prove disastrous and that she should have second thoughts.

Priest

To dream that you are confessing to a priest, implies humiliation caused by unfair publicity. For a young woman to dream that she is in love with a priest, implies that she is placing confidence in a liar.

Prison

To dream of a prison, usually denotes misunderstandings with friends that will cause you stress. To dream of being in prison, denotes troubles and disappointment to the dreamer.

Promenade

To dream that you are promenading, denotes that you will engage in a profitable business. To see others promenading, means keen competition in business lies ahead.

Property

To dream of receiving property as a gift, implies prosperity and ultimate wealth. To dream of losing property, foretells that you will suffer financially from someone failing to follow your instructions.

Prostitute

To dream of being in a prostitute's company, denotes that you will be blamed for things you have done. To dream of being bothered by a prostitute, denotes that you are very popular with the opposite sex and that they think of you as being their idol.

Prunes

To see them on trees, or eat them, denotes joy. Dried prunes relate to problems. To dream of them out of season, obstacles and difficulties, but only for a short duration.

Puddings

To dream of seeing pudding being made, denotes that you will profit from an unlikely investment. To dream that you are eating pudding, means that troubles and disappointments lie ahead.

Pulpit

To dream that you are speaking from a pulpit, or that you are standing in a pulpit, denotes sorrows and discontentment due to poor business dealings and lack of opportunities.

Pulse

To dream that you feel someone's pulse, denotes that your actions will be exposed and publicly criticized. To feel your own pulse, is a sign that you are suffering from stress and need relaxation.

Pump

To dream that you are pumping clear water, means that you will attain much joy and success. To dream of seeing others pumping water, foretells that others who are less successful than you, are jealous of the influence that you wield among your friends.

Punishment

To dream of undergoing punishment, denotes temporary success and wealth. To cause another to be punished, indicates that you enjoy causing spiteful situations for others.

Puppies

To dream of puppies, foretells that you will enjoy many trusted friends. This is especially true if the puppies are healthy and cute. Should they be thin and sickly looking, the reverse of the above would be the case.

Purchase

To dream of making a purchase, denotes that you will forget, or misplace something that you will need badly; however, you will not necessarily lose it.

Purse

To dream of finding a purse containing money and some other valuables, foretells that you will receive money that you are really looking for.

Pyramid

To dream of climbing a pyramid, denotes that you will take a long extended vacation that you've been looking forward to with pleasure. To dream of seeing one, implies wealth and joy and a possible raise in the near future.

"And it shall come to pass afterward, that I will pour out my spirit upon all flesh; and your sons and your daughters shall prophesy, your old men shall dream dreams, your young men shall see visions."

Joel ii, 28

Quail

To dream of quails, is considered a very favorable omen. To dream of killing them, indicates selfishness shown by your friends. To dream of eating them, implies overgenerosity, which should be controlled.

Quarantine

To dream that you are held in quarantine, warns of many spiteful actions taken by vicious people.

Quarrel

To dream of quarreling with a stranger, denotes that you will shortly make a new acquaintance, one who will make you sorry you ever met. To quarrel with a friend, implies that you will soon have a pleasant time with a friend. For lovers to dream of quarreling, predicts that they will be more in love than before.

Quarry

To dream of falling into a quarry, warns that you will have many problems due to your enemies. To dream of working in a quarry, denotes that your success is only gained after much hard work and careful saving.

Quartet

To dream that you belong to, or are singing in a quartet, denotes that harmony and congenial surroundings will make life worthwhile.

Queen

To dream of a queen, is a lucky omen. It speaks of success in recent investments. To dream of one who has lost her beauty, denotes disappointments.

Questions

To dream of asking a question, denotes that your integrity is recognized, and that you will soon be promoted to a trusted position. For you to question another, implies that deceitful friends are trying to hurt you.

Quicksand

To dream of sinking in quicksand, denotes trouble and problems caused by liars. To see others in quicksand, denotes that you will frustrate the plans of someone who is trying to hurt you.

Quinine

To dream of taking quinine, means renewed energy to deal with your problems. To dream of giving it to others, dividends from hopeful prospects will be very small and will remain uncertain.

Quoits

To dream of playing quoits, foretells an ambition that is slow in realization. To see others play, denotes that your success will depend much upon your power of concentration.

R

"And being warned of God in a dream that they should not return to Herod, they departed into their own country another way."

Matthew ii, 12

Rabbits

To dream of rabbits, is good. Conditions are sure to move along smoothly and bring good profits. To the lover, it denotes a proposal through a letter; accept it and happiness is yours. For a married woman to dream of these animals, foretells an increase in the family.

Race

To dream that you are running a race and win, foretells victory in business affairs; to lose in one, implies others are interfering in your efforts.

Radish

To dream of radishes, denotes that your ambition will be swiftly realized. To dream of eating them, warns that you will suffer through someone's deceit.

Rage

To dream that you are in a terrible rage, denotes that you will have quarrels with friends, which may end in bodily harm. To see others carrying on in this manner, denotes that business is slowly declining. For an unmarried woman to dream of being in a rage, implies that she is mistaken if she thinks her lover is faithful.

Railroad

To dream of a railroad, generally refers to travels. If the road is clear, safe trips. To see an obstruction, warns of unpleasant trips, and in business, unfavorable conditions. To dream of walking on a railroad, denotes worries and disappointments lie in the future.

Rain

To dream of being in a soft rain, indicates good things to the dreamer. To dream of being in a terrible rainstorm, warns of losses and irritations to those who are affluent and good things to those who are poor.

Rainbow

To see a rainbow in your dream, omens good things to the dreamer. A lull in business will turn to a more promising aspect. For sweethearts to dream of a rainbow denotes, that their union will bring happiness and contentment.

Raisins

To dream of eating raisins, denotes a realization of wealth and joy. Wealth, however, may come slowly, but it will come, nevertheless.

Ram

To dream of being bucked by a ram, denotes that you will be reprimanded by one for whom you failed to perform requested duties.

Rape

To dream that a person you know has been raped, denotes that you will hear of some scandal surrounding dear friends.

For an unmarried woman to dream that she has been raped, implies that she will hear damaging news relating to the one she loves.

Raspberries

To dream of raspberries in season, is a good omen. To a business man, success due to his own determination and strict attention to business. For an unmarried woman to dream of raspberries, means that her lover will be industrious and a good provider.

Rats

To dream of rats, is a bad sign of loss by theft. To hear them gnawing is unusually bad. When a girl who has a lover dreams of rats, it is a warning for caution in order to protect her honor.

Raven

To dream of ravens, relates to unhappy conditions in business affairs. To kill them, denotes a quarrel due to your defiance and resistance.

Razor

To dream of sharpening a razor for the sole purpose of fighting with another, means conflicts that may prove disastrous. To dream of cutting yourself, you will have enemies to deal with.

Reapers

To dream of seeing reapers in the field busily harvesting an abundant crop, implies prosperity and great joy. To dream of seeing them idle, denotes that your efforts in a current project will yield little success for you at the time but that your fortunes may change later on.

Refrigerator

To dream of a refrigerator, denotes that you will hurt a friend's feelings at a party, by acting selfishly. Rude comments will be made about your behavior and your reputation may suffer.

Reindeer

To dream of this animal, denotes many true and devoted friends. To drive one, denotes a gain in business, through the prestige of people not connected with the business.

Relics

To dream of relics, is a warning to be careful of some household valuable. To dream of receiving a relic, denotes that you will break or spoil something that you value highly.

Reptiles

To dream of reptiles that appear harmless while you watch their graceful movements, denotes settlement of money that you had thought was as good as lost. To dream of seeing them viciously wanting to attack you, implies enemies will renew their bitterness towards you. To dream of killing reptiles, foretells that you will overcome great obstacles. To handle them without harm, omens that the bitterness of friends will be replaced by pleasure and happiness.

Resign

To dream that you have resigned your position, predicts that an advantageous change is in store for you shortly.

Revenge

To dream of revenging yourself, denotes an insensitive nature on your part. This tendency will be the cause of losing many good friends through your insensitivity.

Revolver

To handle a revolver in your dream, is not good. It relates to quarrels and conflict. You should cultivate more self-control. For an unmarried woman to dream of this firearm, denotes an interference with someone she loves.

Rhubarb

To dream of this vegetable, denotes that you are a good-natured person and many people enjoy being in your company to listen to your philosophy. To dream of eating it, means that present plans will end favorably.

Ribbon

To see a display of ribbon in your dreams, denotes a happy and good-natured disposition and that you can put aside your problems when you choose to. For an unmarried woman to dream of ribbons, denotes that her sweetheart is only having a good time, but he'll settle down soon.

Rice

To dream of eating rice, signifies domestic bliss and business success. To see a quantity of rice, implies prosperity in all work aspects and many true friends.

Riches

To dream that you are rich, denotes that your aggressive and firm nature will bring you what you justly deserve.

Rings

To dream of seeing rings on your fingers, implies new plans, which generally turn out well. To see rings sticking in the ground with only the settings visible and pick them out, denotes disappointments, relating to business. For an unmarried woman to receive a ring, means that an old love affair will be revived and end in marriage.

Riot

To see a riot in progress, means disappointments. To dream of seeing someone killed that you know, predicts poor conditions in business.

Rival

To dream of having differences with a rival, denotes that you are weak, indecisive, and afraid to assert your right. To succeed in removing your rival, denotes that you are a splendid leader and that you should seek a leadership position.

River

To dream of a clear and tranquil river, is a lucky omen, particularly for people in a professional calling. To dream of a wavy, rising river, means jealousy and dissatisfaction. To see a river overflow its banks, and the water is clear, denotes meeting a person of distinction. To see muddy water in a similar condition, foretells that lack of interest caused by indiscreet actions of others must be settled.

Road

To dream of following a straight and easy road, denotes joy and prosperity. To be on one that winds and is hard to follow, denotes changes that will be unfavorable.

Rocks

To find yourself climbing on rocks and succeed in reaching the top, denotes joy and happiness. To dream that you fail to reach the top, denotes disappointment and obstacles.

Roof

To dream of being on a roof, indicates success. To have difficulty in getting down, denotes that your success is of an uncertain nature. To dream of seeing others on a roof who are unable to get down, implies petty irritations.

Roosters

To dream of a rooster, is a happy omen; it relates to great success, but the success may have a tendency to make you conceited and unbearable in your actions. You may therefore lose the respect of others.

Ropes

To dream of climbing a rope, and to succeed in reaching the desired spot, means that you will overcome enemies. To fail in climbing the rope successfully, foretells of interferences from someone you have no choice in dealing with. To dream of walking a rope, denotes that you will succeed in some investment. To see others walking a rope, means acquisitions through the kind assistance of friends. To dream of jumping a rope, predicts that you are well liked and respected by those who are your friends.

Roses

To dream of seeing beautiful roses in season, denotes that success is heading your way; it also speaks of happy events.

For an unmarried woman to dream of gathering roses, denotes an early proposal from her ideal.

Rowing

To dream that you are rowing in a boat with others, denotes that you will enjoy the pleasure of happy and knowledgeable associates. Should the boat you are rowing capsize, warns that you may face monetary difficulties due to slow business. To win in a race, honors will be yours. To lose, you will lose your loved one to a rival.

Ruins

To dream of a ruin, implies unexpected acquisitions or fortune. To dream of being among ruins, discoveries leading to success. To dream of ancient ruins, refers to extensive travels in foreign lands.

Running

To dream of running fast, is an excellent omen. Your plans will materialize quickly. To stumble or fall, disappointment. After an enemy, victory; great profit if you catch the enemy. To run naked, trust violated by relatives. For a sick person to dream of running, omens disaster to the dreamer. For a woman to dream of running nude; dishonor and loss of friends will be hers.

S

"And the King said unto them, I have dreamed a dream, and my spirit was troubled to know the dream."

Daniel ii, 3

Safe

To dream of a safe, denotes that your business will prosper without serious problems. To dream of opening, or working the combination of a safe, denotes a disappointment, relating to business matters that you initially believed to be a good investment.

Sailing

To dream that you are out sailing on calm waters, means excellent success in whatever is attempted. To be on wavy, murky water, predicts unpleasant occurrences which will deplete your energies.

Sailor

To dream of seafarers, predicts unpleasant and exciting trips by water. For an unmarried woman to dream of a sailor as her suitor, denotes struggles due to her overanxious desire for admiration.

Salad

To eat salad in your dream, denotes that you will be very bored by disagreeable people. For an unmarried woman to dream of making it, denotes that she should insist on an early marriage because her lover is unpredictable and fickle.

Salmon

To dream of salmon, often refers to troubles in the family. To eat it, predicts arguments with neighbors.

Salt

To dream of salt, foretells of conflicts with close associates. To dream of spilling it, enemies will openly accuse you of a wrongdoing. To an unmarried woman, dreaming of salt means lover's quarrels through jealousy on her part, due to the sweetheart talking about women she dislikes. Don't pay attention to what is said and there will be no argument.

Sash

For a young and unmarried woman to dream of wearing a long sash, denotes that her sweetheart is faithful but conceals his affections for obvious reason.

Satan

To see some form of a satan in your dreams, relates to business plans that may prove futile. To dream that you are fleeing from the devil, denotes that you will conquer your enemies and turn them into your best friends. To dream of being punished by satan, is a warning against believing flatterers who are trying to win your confidence.

Sausage

To dream of making them, is a warning of excessive sexual pleasure. To eat them, means love intrigues.

Saw

Dreaming of saws, in general, is good. To dream that you are working with a saw, predicts activity and energy that will most certainly bring about a comfortable life. To dream of seeing others working with a saw, foretells gains that were thought impossible.

Scaffold

To dream of a scaffold, denotes disappointments that will greatly hurt your dignity. To examine one, implies deceit from those you always trusted.

Scales

To dream that you are weighing yourself on a scale, denotes an increase in your financial situation, and that pending investments will bring flattering results. To see others weighing themselves, indicates that you lack decision and depend too much on others' opinions.

School

To dream that you are young and attending school, indicates distinction in some mental line. To dream of visiting a schoolhouse, where you once attended, implies petty annoyances relating to present business.

Scissors

To dream of scissors, means trouble. For the married, it tells of jealousy and suspicion. To sweethearts, quarrels and accusations; a love that won't run smoothly.

Scratch

To dream that you have a bleeding scratch on you, denotes that enemies are trying to destroy your property; if the scratch does not bleed, their plans will fail and you will enjoy peace and prosperity.

Screech Owl

To dream of hearing the sounds of this owl, implies bereavement, usually the death of a near relative.

Sculptor

To dream of a sculptor, means a change in your profession, generally to one of great importance that will command more respect.

Scythe

To dream of this implement, denotes that some unforeseen circumstances will prevent you from performing your duties properly. To dream of one that is old and worn out, means troubles with friends, due to your bluntness.

Sea

To dream of hearing the roaring of the sea in a storm, foretells a lonely life due to your reserved and self-centered tendencies. To dream of the sea, denotes pleasant and happy travels. For an unmarried woman to dream that she is on a calm sea with her lover, denotes marital happiness.

Seal

To dream of seals, denotes very extravagant tastes that will be the cause of great hardship later in life. It is a warning that your extravagance is abnormal and that you should control it to avoid problems in the future.

Seducer

For an unmarried woman to dream of being seduced, denotes that she is too sentimental and impressionable. The dreamer should cultivate more strength of character and set goals in life. Should a man dream of betraying a girl in this manner, implies that false accusations will be directed against him which will humiliate him.

Seizures

To dream of being afflicted with seizures, is an indication of an illness, which will make you unable to perform your duties. To dream of seeing others suffering from seizures, is a sign of deceit among your fellow workers.

Serenade

To dream of hearing a serenade, denotes that you will receive pleasant and delightful distant news. To help to serenade, splendid things are in store for you.

Serpents

To dream of serpents, generally denotes enemies and ingratitude from friends. To see them curl, twist, and crawl, denotes hatred and illness. To kill them, victories over enemies. To capture one, you'll succeed in destroying jealousy.

Servant

To dream of discharging a servant, implies losses and regretful occurrences. To dream of quarreling with one, denotes that you are too friendly with your servants; show more dignity and make them look up to you.

Sewing

To dream of sewing and altering, denotes disappointment in an anticipated event. To dream of sewing something brand new, means that joy and contentment will be soon be yours.

Shampoo

To dream of seeing someone being shampooed, denotes that you are requested to perform a duty that you consider to be undignified. To dream of having your own hair shampooed, denotes that you must be more secretive, or you will arouse suspicion in others.

Shaving

To dream of being closely shaved, denotes that a friend will help you by paying a loan that is due. To dream of shaving yourself, predicts that you will incur a debt innocently, or perhaps overdraw your bank account.

Sheep (see Lamb)

To dream of seeing a flock of sheep, denotes good luck to the dreamer. To see them thin and sick looking, denotes debts brought about through poor financing. To dream of cutting their wool, rewarded efforts.

Shelter

To dream of seeking shelter from rain, relates to secret problems. To dream of seeking shelter from a storm, denotes that the optimism you now hold for your present plans will turn into despair.

Sheriff

To dream that you succeed in hiding from a sheriff, denotes that you are carrying on illegitimate plans which will be profitable for a short time. To dream of being apprehended by a sheriff, implies that present difficulties will result in more joyful times ahead.

Ship

To dream of seeing a ship in perfect condition, is a good omen. To dream of a ship in great distress in stormy waters, denotes troubles in conducting your business, or that a secret about you will be revealed which will ruin your reputation forever. To see others shipwrecked, means distress over someone's wrongdoings. To dream of being shipwrecked yourself, denotes danger or loss of your reputation.

Shirt

To dream of taking off your shirt, predicts a separation from a loved one, generally due to your inconsiderate actions. To see your shirt torn in your dream, relates to pleasant surprises. To lose it, troubles in business or affairs of the heart. To dream of a soiled shirt, predicts that you are overly stressed and that you need to take a vacation.

Shoes

To dream of shoes that are badly worn or worn down, denotes that you lack tact and are too blunt and outspoken; consequently, you make enemies. To dream of having them shined, omens prosperity and happy events. To see your shoes untied, means disagreements in friendship. New shoes, good news, hope to be realized. For a young woman to dream that a gentleman removed her shoes, denotes that the dreamer must be cautious, for her lover may make sexual overtures toward her.

Shooting

To dream that you are shooting, denotes misunderstandings between friends. To hear shooting, means disagreements in your marriage, and to sweethearts, denotes quarrels of a temporary nature that will be resolved between you and your loved one in the near future.

Shroud

To dream of a shroud, predicts unhappiness and a tendency to illness, from which business may suffer. To dream of seeing a shroud removed, omens arguments and disagreements from a source you least expect.

Sickness

To dream that you are sick, denotes sadness and sorrow. To nurse the sick, joy, profit, and happiness. To see a member of your family sick, an unexpected pleasure that will end in sadness.

Silk

To dream of silk in any form, is a happy sign; your ambition will be achieved, and happiness will replace any present conflict. To dream of silk, also means that you possesses great pride in your work.

Silkworm

To dream of a silkworm, implies that you are thinking about a new investment, which will prove very successful. To see them shedding their cocoons, denotes success after experiencing many obstacles.

Silver

To dream of silverware, implies that the dreamer is too materialistic and takes little interest in the spiritual. Material pleasures seem to be very important. To dream of silver money, implies irritations relating to meeting obligations.

Sing

To dream that you are singing, denotes that your happy moments will become sorrow. To the unmarried, suspicion and jealousy may soon arise and destroy their happy dreams. To hear others sing, omens happy news and pleasant moments spent with cheerful friends.

Skating

To dream of seeing skating, denotes humiliation from those who are jealous of your position by gossiping about you. To dream that you are skating, denotes that you are about to make a change which you will regret. Think twice before you act.

Skeleton

To dream of seeing a skeleton approaching you, foretells sad and shocking news. To dream of seeing a motionless skeleton, implies enemies undermining your efforts.

Skull

To dream of skulls, is a sign of family troubles and a general reminder of one another's shortcomings. To the unmarried, quarrels due to fickle and changeable personalities. To dream of a skull of someone you know, means injured pride.

Sleep

To dream of seeing others sleeping, denotes that you will succeed in accomplishing your objective. To sleep with an ugly person, implies sickness and discontent. For a young woman to dream of sleeping with a handsome man, troubles, irritations, and possible loss of something you love. To sleep with a woman, if married, troubles to your wife, or family; if single, danger of deceptions, or that you will believe the lies told to you by a woman who wants you as her lover. To dream of being discovered with another, denotes disappointment relating to money matters.

Sliding

To dream of sliding down a deep slope, denotes that you are too gullible and may suffer a financial loss by placing too much confidence in a business venture. To slide in general, implies disappointments. To the lover, differences over trivial matters are in store for you.

Smoke

To dream of being in, or suffering from smoke, denotes injury through the schemes of false friends. To see smoke, false glory.

Snail

To see a snail crawl in your dream, relates to an honorable responsibility. To see one with long horns, infidelity, adultery, and fondness for vulgarity. To step on one, you will meet people that you wish you had not.

Snakes

To dream of snakes, as a rule implies misfortune or immorality in some form or other. To dream that a snake bites you, signifies a quarrel with a friend or relative. If a snake winds around you, and you are unable to conquer it, tells of an enemy that will deeply anger you. To dream of being surrounded with these reptiles and succeed in killing one out of many, signifies that someone will cheat you in money matters. To succeed in killing every snake around you, omens that you will have great power over your enemies. To walk over the snakes without trying to kill them, denotes that you are wearing out your nerves by useless worrying and fear. To dream that they bite you, means that you will do something illegal or immoral through enemies. To dream of handling them if they seem playful and harmless, implies that you are inventing a plan to deceive those who oppose you. To step on snakes without being bitten, denotes that you will be bored by those you thought were interesting.

Snow

To dream that you are in a snowstorm, denotes disappointment regarding a pleasure that you had been looking forward to with great enthusiasm. To dream of seeing dirty snow, predicts that your pride will suffer and that you will acknowledge those you once thought were beneath you. To dream of being snowbound, means that many obstacles and hard work lie ahead. To see a few inches of beautiful snow on the ground, denotes joy and pleasure. To eat snow or to taste it, means good health will be yours.

Soldier

To dream that you are a soldier, means that your ambition will be achieved. To see a wounded solider, denotes that the distressing condition of others has aroused your sympathy and will cause you to fight against them despite your better judgment. To see them marching, means a promotion for you. For an unmarried woman to dream of a solider, is a warning to resist immoral propositions.

Son

For a father to dream of his son looking healthy, or anything that is favorable about him, denotes that he will make his mark in the world and gain great honor for his outstanding qualities. For a mother to dream favorably about her son, the above interpretation can be used. To dream of him in pain, refers to grief, loss, and sorrow.

Soup

To dream of eating soup, foretells comfort and happiness. To see others eating it, few obstacles in your attempts.

Sowing

To dream of seeing others sowing, indicates an advancement in business matters. To dream of yourself sowing, denotes hopes to be realized.

Sparrow

To dream of sparrows, denotes that neighbors are jealous of your possessions or begrudge your success.

Spider

To see spiders in your dreams, denotes that thrifty and conscientious tendencies will be the key to acquiring a large fortune. To dream of killing one, signifies quarrels and hatred. For a young woman to dream of having a pet spider, predicts that she will marry a professional man.

Splinter

To dream of having a splinter in your body, denotes that you will be annoyed by friends.

Spoons

To dream of a spoon, indicates marital happiness and contentment. To dream that you are stealing a spoon, denotes that your company manners do not correspond with your at-home manners.

Squirrel

To see squirrels in your dream, denotes a pleasant surprise, also rising business conditions. To dream of having one for a pet, happiness and contentment. To kill one, signifies a lack of tact on your part.

Stags

To dream of stags, implies that you have many true friends and your power behind the scene is in much demand at gatherings and organizations.

Stallion

To see a fine stallion in your dream, implies that you will achieve honor and riches. To dream of riding a gentle one, you'll gain much distinction locally.

Stars

To dream of seeing clear and brilliant stars, tells of good news, prosperity, and pleasant trips. Shooting or falling stars, on the other hand, mean that sorrow lies ahead.

Starving

To dream of seeing others in a starved condition, implies problems and financial difficulties. To dream that you suffer from starvation, unexpected good fortune.

Statuary

To dream of sculptured figures, denotes that a gift will come from someone you thought had lost all respect for you.

Stealing

To dream of catching a woman in the act of stealing and holding her until a policeman arrives, but through her smiling and innocent expression the officer refuses to arrest her and sets her free, indicates that you will reveal a secret of your past life that some day you will greatly regret. To dream that you have stolen something and afterwards are discovered with stolen property, but return it to the owner and all is forgiven, denotes that you will receive unexpected money. To accuse others of stealing, denotes that you lack consideration towards others by your actions.

Steeple

To dream of seeing a high steeple on a church, implies an uncertain physical condition, a warning to the dreamer of an illness. To dream of climbing one, and succeed in reaching the top, success and honor. To fail to reach the top, many difficulties of various kinds.

Stillborn

To dream of a stillborn birth, relates to discouraging incidents and many things to distract your attention from regular work routine.

Stilts

To see others walking on stilts, means uncertainties in business conditions. To be walking on stilts yourself, denotes an opposition from others relating to a plan that you have proposed to them for their approval.

Sting

To feel the sting of an insect in your dream, implies unhappiness due to rigid demands from others.

Stockings

For a woman to dream of beautiful stockings, denotes that she is fond of admiration and encourages men's attention through her actions. To see her stockings torn, denotes that she will do whatever is necessary to gain financial reward; a warning, to resist temptation.

Store

To dream of a large store filled with goods, indicates success through rapid advancement. To dream of being in a large store, pleasure and good fortune. To dream of working in one, your success is brought about through your own personal efforts and hard work.

Storm

To dream of hearing the howling of a storm, and if the storm causes destruction, means business troubles and disagreements with friends. Should the storm pass by without causing any damage, the above indication will be greatly improved and your outlook, better.

Strawberries

To dream of strawberries tells of success in love and a happy marriage. To eat them, honor and security in business.

Street

To dream of wandering in a street aimlessly, denotes mental anxiety, and that you may become discouraged with your job. To dream that you are walking the street in a happy mood, means that your desired goal will be realized. To dream of being on a dark street and to experience fear, but not to be molested, denotes that you will achieve great success after your strenuous efforts.

Struggling

To dream that you are engaged in a struggle, means that difficulties to overcome lie ahead. To dream of coming out victorious, signifies success due to your firm determination.

Suffocating

To dream that you are suffocating, implies sorrow due to the coldness and indifference of someone you deeply love. To see others suffocating, you are being imposed upon due to your kind nature.

Sugar

To dream of eating sugar, denotes that you will experience things that are not as pleasant as you imagined they would be, but your perseverance will help you in working toward your goal.

Suicide

To dream of suicide, denotes that your reserved and self-centered tendencies cause people to misjudge you. To see another commit suicide, means that others' losses and reversals of fortune may directly affect you.

Sun

To dream of seeing a bright sun, denotes discovery of secrets for the growth of business. To see the sun rise, good news. To see it setting, false news pertaining to losses. To dream of the sun, is considered a good sign for those who have problems, or who must deal with their enemies.

Surgical Instruments

To see these instruments in your dream, denotes worry and outlay of money due to illness, and accidents that may occur in the family.

Swan

To dream of large and beautiful white swans on clear and quiet waters, foretells prosperity and pleasant occurrences. To dream of black swans on muddy and troubled waters, means that pleasure will bring disgrace and loss of reputation.

Swearing

To dream of hearing others swearing, indicates obstacles in business. To lovers, interferences in their love life.

Sweetheart

To dream that your sweetheart has a pleasant and good-natured personality, indicates that your marriage will be a happy one, not filled with yelling or arguments. To dream of a sweetheart that is unpleasant and opinionated, happiness will vanish and an end to a relationship is probable.

Swimming

To dream that you are swimming in clear water with skill and ease, speaks of success in your business. To dream of swimming underwater, or that you bob up and down, omens struggles and humiliations.

Sword

To dream of wearing a sword is good; it relates to distinction. To dream that a friend hands you a broken sword, indicates trouble with the law, where your defense will be ignored and you will receive little or no compassion. To dream of seeing many swords, indifferences to be resolved.

T

"And it came to pass at the end of the two full
years, that Pharaoh dreamed; and behold, he stood
by the river."

Genesis xii, I

Table

To dream of a table full of appetizing foods, denotes the
indulgence of pleasures. To dream of clearing a table,
implies pleasures that will wind up in difficulties. To dream
of eating from a table, means happiness and comfortable circumstances. To dream of breaking one, disappointment.

Tail

To dream of seeing the tail of an animal, implies annoyance over trivial things. To dream that you possess a long tail
similar to that of an animal, foretells a gloomy outlook relating to a new project. To dream of cutting a tail, means that
you should think before you speak tactlessly in public.

Tailor

To dream of a tailor measuring your body for clothing,
implies pleasant surprises. To dream of a tailor at work
denotes confusion connected with your duties. To have trouble with a tailor, small losses of some kind.

Talisman

To dream of receiving this type of a charm, means profits
due to the honest advice of a friend. For an unmarried

woman to dream of receiving a charm, indicates that her lover has decided she is the only one for him.

Talking

To dream of someone who acts as if he wants to talk with you, but doesn't, denotes that nothing will become of a seemingly good idea. To dream that you are talking to others, denotes worrying prematurely. To hear people talk, or feel that they are talking about you, predicts that you will be accused of contributing to the downfall of another.

Tambourine

To dream of seeing others using this instrument, or hear its sounds, denotes pleasant surprises mixed with a gradual increase in business. To dream of dancing to one, means great delight is yours to enjoy.

Tapestry

To dream of seeing beautiful tapestries, denotes culture and refinement, and that you are extravagant in your taste. To dream of possessing them, wealth will be acquired. For an unmarried woman to dream of them, a brilliant marriage.

Tapeworm

To dream of suffering with a tapeworm, denotes that you are nervous, restless, excitable, and let imagined illness influence you needlessly. To see one, disappointment.

Tar

To dream of having tar on your hands, or on your clothes, denotes disappointments and irritations. To see it in large quantities, troubles caused by enemies.

Tattoo

To dream of seeing someone tattooed, denotes that the success of others will hurt your feelings and minimize your abilities. To see yourself tattooed, implies family separations.

Taxes

To dream of being unable to meet your taxes, or feel that they are too high, denotes that you will be excessively pressured to fulfill an obligation. To pay them and feel satisfied, denotes hopes to be realized.

Tea

To dream of tea in general, denotes financial difficulties that are a drain on your assets, which are worrying you. To drink it, pleasures that will create problems. To see others drink it, you will be asked to help someone in trouble.

Tears

To dream that you are overcome by emotion and cry, means sorrow. To see others in tears, others will be sympathetic to your suffering.

Teasing

To dream of teasing another, means that your friends think that you are clever, and come to you for advice. To dream of being teased, means that joy, contentment, and future popularity lie ahead for you.

Teeth

To dream of having false teeth and taking them out of your mouth, implies dental work that will either be painful or unsatisfactory. To dream that your teeth are worn down to the gums, denotes quarrels that will end in disgrace with a close associate. To dream that your teeth are loose, unpleasant things to cope with. To lose them, hardship will rob you of your pride. To have them examined, a warning to be careful of enemies. To dream of having poor teeth, money troubles. To spit them out, illness and sorrow in the family. To dream of one tooth being longer than the others, pain caused by a parent. To have one fall out, sad news. To dream that your teeth are white and beautiful, when, in reality, they are not, joy, health, and prosperity. To dream that your teeth are so long that they annoy you, quarrels and possible lawsuits.

Telegram

To dream of sending a telegram, predicts that you will have difficulties with a very close friend who, in turn, will criticize your business. To dream of receiving one, is an indication that you will receive profitable news.

Telephone

To dream of talking on the telephone, denotes rivals, both in business and in love.

Tempest

To dream of a tempest, implies controversies with friends; misfortune is also predicted. To dream of being knocked down by a tempest, denotes malicious planning among your enemies.

Temptation

To dream of resisting temptation, means trouble of some kind. If you succeed in resisting temptation, success will come after much hard work.

Tent

To dream of a city of tents, signifies changes in region. To dream of being in a tent, means a change in business. If the tent is strong and secure, the change will be good.

Terror

To dream of being terrorized by something, denotes disappointment. To see others terrorized, sad news from friends.

Thaw

To dream of seeing ice thaw, relates to pleasure and profit. To dream that it is thawing from beneath you, denotes energies directed in the wrong direction.

Theater

To dream of being in a theater, relates to pleasant and congenial friends. To dream that you are an actor in a theater, denotes an early change in your situation which will prove profitable. To dream of being in one during a fire, signifies a change that will not be profitable.

Thief

To dream of thieves entering your house and robbing you, denotes profit and honor. To dream of catching a thief and arresting him, indicates shrewdness on your part in deceiving your enemies. To dream that you are a thief and are being chased by police, denotes business troubles.

Thighs

To dream of admiring your thighs, indicates pleasure and good cheer. For a young woman to admire her thighs, predicts that her foolishness and selfishness may cause her to make wrong decisions resulting in unhappiness.

Thirst

To feel thirsty in your dream, denotes that you are very ambitious and love leadership. To dream of quenching your thirst, your love for leadership will be rewarded.

Thorns

To dream of seeing thorns, denotes that your neighbors are envious towards you. To dream that thorns are on your body, you will be harassed. To dream of being pricked with them, troubles with the dreamer's employment.

Thread

To dream of unraveling thread, denotes discovery of a secret. To dream of tangling it, you will tell a secret to an indiscreet friend and it will become public knowledge.

Threshing

To dream that you assist in threshing a huge amount of grain, denotes a prosperous business and joy. To see others threshing, you will enjoy great pleasure from the generosity and wealth of others.

Throat

To dream of cutting another's throat, denotes that you will injure a person accidentally. To dream that your throat is cut, hopes and success will be shattered. To dream of a well-leveloped throat, success will be achieved in the near future. To dream of having a sore throat, anxiety.

Thunder

To hear thunder in your dream, is a warning that troubles will endanger your business. To hear thunder and see vivid lightning flash, loss of wealth.

Tiger

To dream of a tiger, denotes jealous and furious enemies. To succeed in warding one off, efforts to be achieved. To kill one, complete success.

Tipsy

To dream that you are tipsy, denotes that you are very optimistic and take life as it comes. To dream of seeing others tipsy, denotes that you are too thoughtless of the future.

Toads

To dream of toads, omens misfortune of some kind. To kill one, implies that you are too impetuous and reckless. To play with one, you will be misjudged by a friend.

Tobacco

To dream of tobacco, is a happy omen. To dream of smoking tobacco, foretells much pleasure. To chew it, means good news is to be expected. To see it grow, denotes success in business.

Tomatoes

To dream of tomatoes, is a good omen. To dream of eating them, splendid health. To gather them, happiness in marriage. For the unmarried to dream of tomatoes, means a happy marriage lies in their future.

Tomb

To see a tomb in your dreams, denotes regrets. To help build one, birth of children. To fall into one, sickness and misery in the family. To read the inscription on one, you'll have to perform duties that are unpleasant.

Tongue

To dream that you see your tongue, or that your tongue is very large, means that you are misunderstood and accused of something you did not do. To dream of seeing someone's tongue, you will hear gossip maligning your character.

Torture

To dream that you assist in torturing others, denotes that plans you thought favorable will prove unsuccessful. To dream of defending others from torture, success after much hard work. To dream that you are tortured yourself, implies sorrow due to actions of deceptive friends.

Tragedy

To dream of a tragedy, denotes friends and wealth. To dream that you contributed to, or were involved in a tragedy, implies personal miseries and profound regret.

Train

To dream that you are riding on a train, implies good news relating to a contemplated project. To dream of attempting to board a train on time, but just missing it, denotes that present complications will ultimately prove beneficial to you. To dream of being on top of a train, and reach your destination successfully, achievements and prosperity.

To drop off, or to fail to reach the desired destination, disappointments and irritations.

Trap

To dream of catching game in a trap, denotes success. To dream of being caught in a trap, enemies will succeed in their plans. To set a trap yourself, implies that your plans or deceptive actions will be discovered.

Traveling

To dream of traveling on foot, denotes a great deal of hard work lies ahead. To dream of traveling by horse-drawn carriage, profit and pleasure combined. To dream of traveling by train, hopes to be realized; by water, prosperity and happiness. To dream of traveling pleasantly without incident, denotes favorable conditions.

Trees

To dream that you are climbing a tree and reach the top easily, means that you are lucky. To fail, an obstacle to cope with. To fall from a tree, misery and sickness. To see green trees, hopes to be realized. To cut one down, senseless spending of money.

Tricks

To dream of seeing tricks performed, denotes fun and happy surprises. To dream of card tricks and that you can detect the trick, business matters will improve.

Triplets

To see triplets in your dream, foretells that your judgment is good and is a warning for you to continue with your plans.

Trophy

To dream of trophies that you have won, or that were presented to you, implies an achievement gained through pleasant and courteous behavior.

Trousers

To dream that you put trousers on inside out, denotes forming an attachment that will be hard to resist. To dream of trousers, refers to secrets which may never be revealed to you.

Trumpet

To hear the blowing of a trumpet, denotes startling news that is nearby. To blow it yourself, ambition to be achieved.

Trunk

Trunks, as a rule, relate to trips. To dream of packing your trunk, you are soon to make a trip. To dream that your trunk is too small, you are to be promoted shortly. To see your clothes scattered all over the trunk instead of being inside, you will change to a place which will dissatisfy you, and will return, sorry you changed in the first place.

Tunnel

To dream of going through a tunnel while on a train, omens an illness and a possible change in business. To dream of being in a tunnel and meeting a train, foretells unhappy conditions relating to business. To dream of being in a tunnel and there meet with difficulties, is always a bad dream.

Turnips

To dream of seeing a large turnip patch, means that circumstances will soon improve. To dream of eating turnips, foretells mild illness to the dreamer. To prepare a dish made with turnips, means that success due to your self-made abilities is imminent.

Turpentine

To dream of seeing turpentine, means unhappiness in the near future. To dream of using it on someone for medical purposes, denotes those whom you've helped owe you a great deal of gratitude.

Twins

To dream of healthy twins, means business success and many happy hours at home. To dream of sickly twins, means sorrow and unhappiness.

U

"And Joseph dreamed a dream, and he told it his brethren; and they hated him yet the more."

Genesis xxxvii, 5

Ugly

To dream of being ugly, signifies misunderstandings between loved ones. In business, things are inclined to drag. For a woman to dream of being unattractive, signifies that her cold and indifferent action will cause her friends to think less of her.

Umbrella

To dream of umbrellas, means that petty problems will ultimately come to a head and annoy you very much. To dream of lending one, destroyed confidence. To borrow one, you will distrust a friend which will ultimately bring about an end to your friendship. To dream of having the storm turning it inside out, denotes irritations from others who want to belittle your reputation.

Uncle

To dream of your uncle, relates to unpleasant news. To dream of seeing your uncle suffering or in a bad situation, denotes family quarrels.

Undress

To dream of seeing others undress, denotes that your joy and satisfaction will end in an uncertainty. To see yourself undress, you will learn bad reports about yourself. For a woman to dream of undressing in the presence of others, denotes that lies regarding her conduct will annoy her greatly and cause her much dismay.

Uniform

To dream of wearing a uniform, denotes distinction in your vocation or career. For a young woman to dream of wearing a uniform, implies a wealthy and happy marriage.

Urgent

To dream that you are helping the continuance of an urgent appeal, predicts involvements from which you may find difficulty in removing yourself

Urn

To dream of urns, denotes that you will turn a struggling business into great success, much to the surprise of others. If they are broken, troubles in business.

Usurper

To dream that you are seizing, or holding property illegally, denotes that you will have trouble over possessions, or in establishing good credit. To dream that others are usurping your rights, implies keen competition in business that will test your skills in learning how to win.

"When he was set down on the judgment seat, his wife
sent unto him, saying, 'Have thou nothing to do with
that just man; for I have suffered many things this
day in my dream, because of him.' "

Matthew xxvii, 19

Vaccinate

To dream of seeing others vaccinated, denotes that you
are too easily lead by flattery and seldom think until it is too
late. To dream of being vaccinated yourself, denotes that the
finger of suspicion will be pointed at you, and it will be difficult for you to prove your innocence. For a woman to dream
of being vaccinated on the leg, denotes lies regarding her
character are being told by others.

Vagrant

To dream of seeing vagrants, denotes fear from a report
of illness in the community. To help, or feed one, many
happy returns. To dream that you are one, obstacles and
annoyances to overcome.

Valentine

To dream of receiving a valentine, denotes disappointments relating to the heart. To send them, means that you
will let good opportunities slip through your fingers.

Valise

To dream of finding a valise, denotes prosperity. To lose
one, sorrow and many struggles in reaching your goal.

Varnish

To see others varnishing in your dream, means irritations through the interferences of others in your daily duties. To varnish yourself, your thrifty and economical qualities are highly appreciated by your superiors.

Vase

To dream of a beautiful vase, denotes many happy conditions to surround you in your future. To dream that you drop a vase and break it, shattered hopes, relating to business plans. For a woman to dream of receiving a vase as a gift, implies that her ambitions will be achieved and rewarded.

Vault

To dream of a vault containing money, signifies that your conduct and way of living puzzles many and has them wondering about you. To dream of a vault for the dead, sad news and things going wrong in general.

Vegetables

To dream of eating vegetables, is an indication of unstable conditions. You may think that you are on solid footing, and all of a sudden, things may go in an opposite direction. These uncertainties are generally caused by those you sincerely trusted. To dream of decayed vegetables, denotes disappointments. To dream of preparing them for a meal, implies that success will come gradually, but surely.

Vehicle

To dream that you are thrown from a vehicle, means that gossip will irritate you and that you will stop at nothing to find its source. To ride in a vehicle successfully and without suffering from any mishap, denotes that you will be victorious over resistance caused by others.

Veil

To dream of a veil in general, denotes that you are not as sincere with friends as you might be. To dream of losing a veil, means a disagreement with a man. To see a bridal veil in your dream, denotes a change that will be lucky. To dream of wearing a bridal veil, predicts an affair that will be completed successfully. To dream of mourning veils, means disappointments and troubles.

Veins

To dream of seeing bleeding veins, denotes sorrows and troubles that will not end.

Velvet

To dream of velvet, is a happy omen; it predicts much happiness to the dreamer. For an unmarried woman to dream that she is wearing a velvet dress, denotes many suitors will love her and ask her to marry them.

Ventriloquist

To dream that you are a ventriloquist, denotes that people distrust you and are afraid to deal with you. To dream of listening to a ventriloquist, denotes that you must be more careful of what you say in public.

Vermin

To dream of seeing vermin crawling about, means worries due to sickness. To dream that you succeed in exterminating it, denotes victory in an attempt.

Vice

To dream that you are encouraging vice in any form, denotes that you are in danger of losing your reputation.

Victim

To dream that you are a victim of another's clever actions, denotes that others will seek to injure you. To dream that you victimize another, implies wealth gained by unquestionable manners.

Victory

To dream that you are victorious in any contest, denotes that you will outsmart your enemies to their great surprise.

Vine

To dream of creeping vines, is a happy omen. If they contain blossoms, the sick will recover and those in good health will be more rugged and vitalized. To dream of vines that are poisonous, means a rundown vitality should be taken care of in order to avoid unhappiness.

Vinegar

To dream of vinegar in general, denotes difficulties or obstacles of some kind. To dream of drinking it, means worries and duties to perform that are not pleasant.

Vineyard

To dream of being in a vineyard with all its ripe fruit, denotes joy as the result of successful investment. To the lover, it predicts an early marriage. To dream of a vineyard with fruit that is out of season, is not a lucky sign.

Violets

To dream of violets, is a splendid sign. For an unmarried woman to gather them, denotes that she will soon meet her future husband. To dream that you gather great quantities of them, means fame and riches.

Violin

To dream of seeing someone playing the violin and that the music is harmoniously sweet, denotes to the businessman that pending investments will turn into unexpected good fortune. For an unmarried woman to dream of playing music on a violin, means that her aspiration will be achieved to the height of her ambition.

Virgin

To dream of a virgin, is very lucky; it denotes success in many directions. For an unmarried woman to dream that she is no longer a virgin, denotes that she will jeopardize her reputation by becoming or acting too intimate with male associates. For a married woman to dream that she is still a virgin, denotes that certain conditions will bring about her past and will cause regret. For a man to dream of seducing a virgin, predicts that his plans relating to the development of business will be slow.

Visit

To dream that you are visiting, is a happy omen; more so if the visit has been pleasant. To dream that a friend visits you, omens good news from someone you like. To dream of receiving a visit from someone who appears in distress, means struggles and disappointment.

Visions

To have someone that you know appear in a vision, relates to troubles in your family. To dream of having strange and confused visions confront you, denotes an illness.

Voices

To hear calm, pleasant voices in your dreams, denotes pleasure and contentment. Should the voices be unpleasant or angry, disappointments are signaled to the dreamer. To hear crying voices, is a warning to be careful of what you say in a fit of anger.

Volcano

To dream of an erupting volcano, means differences that have to be resolved. The dreamer should be very careful after such a dream regarding what is said to those with whom you have differences.

Vomit

To see others vomiting in your dream, denotes that you will be harassed by lies about you. To dream that you are vomiting, implies that there is danger of an illness for you.

Vote

To dream of voting, denotes a petition in your community on which your signature is solicited. To dream of being paid to vote a certain way, or for a certain party, means that you will take a step against your better judgment.

Vow

To dream that you see someone making any sort of vow, denotes a complaint in regard to the handling of your affairs.

To dream of taking a vow, or making a vow yourself, foretells deceit and delusion.

Vultures

To dream of vultures, generally refers to prolonged illnesses, sometimes to enemies that are trying to harm you.

"Dreams are prophetic and cast their shadows of coming events before."

Wading

To dream of wading in clear water, denotes joy and pleasure is certain to be yours.

Wager

To dream of betting, denotes that you will resort to cheating in order to make your plans succeed. To lose a wager, implies that illegal actions are being committed by those who dislike you.

Wages

To dream of receiving wages, means a change to your advantage. To dream of an increase in wages, profitable undertakings. To have them reduced, unpleasant things from those you highly respected.

Wagon

To dream of a wagon, warns of dissatisfaction in general. To dream of getting into a wagon, means shame due to an unfortunate accident. To dream of getting out of one, loss and a possible struggle to keep what is rightfully yours. To dream of riding down a hill, hope to be furthered. Uphill, discouragement, relating to work. To drive over an embankment, implies sorrow and grief. To dream that you are driving very close to the edge of a cliff, denotes some illegal involvement over which you will be very annoyed and from which you must disassociate yourself.

Waiter

To dream that a waiter is pleasantly serving you, denotes happy hours spent in the presence of friends. To see one who is inattentive, gives poor service, and is grumpy, means that you will be bored by friends.

Walking

To dream that you are walking and rejuvenated, denotes consolation and happiness. To dream of walking and to find it difficult to continue, implies troubles and pain. To walk in the night, implies struggles and complications.

Wallet

To dream of finding a wallet with money, denotes good fortune. To find an empty one, worry and problems.

Walls

To dream of coming to a wall and being unable to pass, denotes difficulties in convincing others of your way of thinking. To dream that you jump over one, you will be able to overcome all obstacles and reach your ambition. To dream that you are walking on top of a high wall with perfect ease, foretells success in your business in the future.

Walnut

To dream of walnuts, is a happy omen. To dream of opening them, or eating them, means difficulties followed by wealth and satisfaction. To dream of gathering them, discovery of a treasure.

Want

To dream of seeing others in want or need, implies dissatisfaction in services rendered by others. To dream that you are in want or need, denotes that you are too thoughtless of the future; you should form a plan for steadily increasing your savings for the future.

War

To see war going on in your dream, denotes arguments within your immediate family. To dream that you are in war, denotes persecution. For a young woman to dream that her sweetheart is going to war, means scandal relating to a near friend.

Wardrobe

To dream of having a large, splendid wardrobe, denotes profit and rapid strides forward. To dream of having a poor wardrobe, means that you are displeased with your community and the people around you.

Warts

To dream of seeing warts on your person, means an annoyance, or that you are unable to get out of a certain thing, or affair. To dream of seeing them on others, is a sign of unknown enemies around you.

Washing

To dream of washing, denotes that some personal interest will suffer through misjudgment. To dream of washing your body or face, means that you may have to forget your pride to ask for a certain thing, or favor.

Wasp

To dream of wasps, denotes enemies that are trying to malign you. To dream that they sting you, you will be very annoyed to learn what your enemies have done.

Watch

To dream that you break a watch, denotes that trouble is ahead of you. To see watches in your dream, relates to successful investments. To dream of receiving a watch, pleasant recreations.

Water

To dream of being in, or on turbulent waters, denotes a disappointment, relating to a deal. To dream of crossing a muddy stream, means troubles collecting money that is due you. To dream of throwing small stones into water so clear that you can see them sink to the bottom, denotes that you will receive something that you have been anxiously awaiting. To dream of seeing clear water, is always good. Muddy water always foretells gloom and disappointment. To dream of seeing water rise so high that it comes into your house, denotes a great struggle in resisting something immoral. To dream of falling into water that is muddy, predicts that you will suffer from many mistakes. To dream of drinking water that is not clear, foretells sickness. To dream of drinking clear water, health.

Waterfall

To see a nice clear waterfall in your dream, denotes that your ambitions will be realized, and that you will live in wealth in years to come.

Waves

To dream of seeing clear waves, denotes pleasure and the accumulation of wisdom. To see them muddy and choppy, losses from poor judgment.

Wealth

To dream of wealth, or see others wealthy, denotes the sincerity of friends that would help you should you have financial problems. To dream that you are very wealthy, predicts that your stamina and aggression will help you attain your goal. For an unmarried woman to dream that her associates are wealthy, implies that she has high ideals and that there is a good possibility of having them realized.

Weaving

To dream of trouble-free weaving, your painstaking efforts will prove rewarding. If accidents occur while weaving, such as the ends entangling or the loom breaking, struggles in your undertakings lie in the future. To see others weaving, favorable conditions will surround you.

Wedding

To dream of a wedding, foretells an early approach of discontent and bitterness. To dream that you are married secretly, discovery of gossip attacking your character. To dream that there are oppositions to your wedding, denotes jealous rivals.

Wedding Clothes

To see wedding clothes in your dream, whether they are the bride's, groom's or attendants' garments, denotes that you will sincerely and pleasantly perform your duties, and that you will meet new and interesting friends.

Wedding Ring

To dream of a wedding ring, denotes that your future life will be a pleasant one with very little chance of unhappiness.

Wedlock

For a woman to dream that she is unhappy in her marriage, denotes that she will hear many disagreeable things, and that others have a compulsion to watch her too closely. To dream of divorcing, denotes disappointment, grief, and many petty jealousies.

Weeping

To dream that you are crying, generally brings sad news, or upheavals in your immediate family. To dream of seeing others cry, denotes hope and joy, after many controversies. To the unmarried, to dream of weeping, means that there are troubles in love to be suffered.

Wet

To dream of being wet, is often a warning to take care of your physical welfare, since exposure or overheating may cause illness. For a woman to dream of being wet to the skin, means trouble and disgrace that can result from being in an illegal relationship.

Whale

To dream of seeing a large whale causing destruction, denotes struggles and possible loss of property.

Wheat

To dream of seeing it in its ear, denotes profit and wealth for you. To see it in large quantities, great wealth. To see large fields of wheat, encouraging prospects. To see it in sacks, ambition will be achieved. To see it in a granary, but diminishing gradually, enemies may be plotting to harm you.

Wheels

To stare at rapidly moving wheels in your dream, denotes success in business and that family matters will resolve themselves. To set, or fix, broken wheels, relates to a disappointment in business matters.

Whip

To dream of a whip or hear the cracking of a whip, means difficulties and many things that need resolution.

Whirlpool

To see a whirlpool in your dream, predicts troubles in business and that the dreamer will suffer from mental stress. If the whirlpool is dirty, enemies may cause problems.

Whirlwind

To dream that you are caught in a whirlwind, denotes that you will not like the change that will take place soon.

Whiskey

To dream of whiskey in any form, denotes that you will push your selfish tendencies so far that your friends will dislike you. To dream of drinking it, many struggles before you reach your desired goal. To see others drinking it, money gained through much scheming.

Whistle

To dream that you are whistling, denotes that you are looking forward to an event centered around you, and where others will criticize you unjustly. To hear others whistle, predicts that you will be opposed in a prospective plan, by friends who are playing a joke on you.

Widow

To dream of being a widow, denotes troubles and many annoying things being said by others. For a man to dream that he marries a widow, means shattered hopes and prevented ambition will cause him sorrow.

Wife

To see your wife in your dream, denotes domestic troubles, generally due to jealousy by your wife. To dream that your wife is lovable and agreeable, success in business. To dream of fighting with your wife, or abusing her, there is cause for the wife's suspicion. For a husband to dream that his wife is in the embrace of another, means a disappointing business proposition will be presented.

Wig

To dream that you are forced to wear a wig due to loss of hair, predicts that you will be influenced to make a change that you'll regret. To see others wearing them, you are being wished bad luck.

Wild

To dream that you are turning wild, means misfortune through some careless act. To see others in this state, mental disturbance and senseless conditions.

Will

To dream of making your will, denotes depression and problems. To dream that a will is made in someone else's favor instead of yours, quarrels of a shameful nature. To dream that you made a will and then destroyed it, predicts that there is trouble coming, which should surface soon.

Wind

To dream that you hear gusty winds blowing loudly, predicts anxieties and mental stress caused by competitors. To dream that wind keeps blowing you backwards, disappointment relating to some cherished hope.

Windmill

To dream of seeing a windmill, denotes attainment of honor, influential position in your community, and wealth.

Window

To dream of open windows, denotes secret schemes under your very nose. To see them closed, you will be denied something you desperately want. To dream of jumping through a window, predicts trouble nearby. To dream of slipping in through a window, possibility of a lawsuit.

Wings

To dream that you have wings and are able to fly, denotes that you take and shoulder the troubles of others too often; consequently, you worry too much needlessly.

Winter

To dream of winter when, in reality, that is not the season, denotes that the dreamer will encounter a slight loss.

This minor loss will be brought about through the suffering of a mild illness, from which the dreamer will fully recover in a short period of time.

Wire

To dream of being caught, or entangled in a wire, denotes that others are afraid of you because you are so stern. To see rusty wire in your dream, denotes troubles due to an uncontrollable temper.

Witch

To dream of witches, denotes that a lull in business is causing you dissatisfaction, and that you are searching for opportunities to improve conditions.

Wizard

To see an individual who claims to work wonders in your dream, denotes that you will be annoyed not only in business, but in public affairs as well.

Wolf

To dream that wolves are following you while you are driving, but they are unable to harm you, signifies success in business. To dream that you kill one, foretells that those whom you trust will deceive you, by failing to make good on promises given. To see a pack of wolves, you love to win through sharp scheming.

Woman

To dream that you quarrel or slap a woman, denotes a disappointment in someone whom you desperately wanted to meet. To dream of seeing a woman hiding, warns that an unprincipled person is taking advantage of your good reputation by passing himself off as your associate. To dream that a woman is watching you, denotes that a former misunderstanding will be straightened out. To dream of committing adultery, means that the person you were once intimate with, will cause a lot of problems. To see a pregnant woman, means receiving pleasant news. To see one with a beautiful figure, joy and satisfaction, if the dreamer is a man. To a woman, this dream means jealousy, arguments, and scandal. To dream of seeing a woman quarrel, disappointment.

Wool

To dream of seeing wool, means slow, but sure prosperity and that you will attain influential prominence in your community. Should the wool be in unuseable condition, this foretells of differences that will not coincide with others and you will be called stubborn.

Work

To dream of seeing others at work, denotes money gained after hard work and concern. To dream that you are at work yourself, denotes success after having tried many different things, for past experiences have forced reality on you.

Worms

To dream of seeing worms on or near your body, denotes little ambition, lack of self-reliance, and easily discouraged characteristics. To dream of killing them, predicts that you will determine to build character in this direction. To use them for fishing purposes, you will make some sudden gain greatly to the surprise of friends.

Wound

To dream of seeing others wounded, predicts an injury, or actions taken to hurt you by seemingly good friends. To have a wound yourself, means business troubles and many things will annoy you.

Wrecks

To dream of seeing a wreck, denotes many distressing obstacles and setbacks in business and that you may look for another career.

Wreath

To dream of a wreath that is fresh and pretty, denotes success and prosperity. To see one that is withered, predicts illness, or unhappiness caused by loved ones.

Writing

To dream that you see others write, denotes accusations from those you tried to please. To write yourself, denotes a miscalculation that will probably cause a loss in business. To read writing, watch those that are trying to interest you in new schemes.

X

"Was it a vision, or a waking dream? Fled is that
music:—Do I wake or sleep?"

KEATS—*Poems. Ode to a Nightingale*

X Ray

The dream of having an x ray taken of your teeth or other
part of your body, foretells of a mysterious occurrence in the
life of one of your friends. If you dream of looking at your
own bones by means of the x ray, you will be called to
account for an indiscretion you have committed.

Xylophone

To dream of playing a xylophone or hearing one played in
a dream, is a sign that you will take part in a pageant of his-
torical interest. If the xylophone is played out of tune, it foretells an accident.

Y

"God came to Laban, the Syrian, by night, in a dream,
and said unto him, take heed that thou speak not to
Jacob, either good or bad."

Genesis xxxi, 24

Yacht

To dream of seeing a yacht, denotes optimism and foresight, and that your efforts are strengthened, or reinforced with recreation. To see one in distress, denotes that business compels you to disappoint friends who are planning a vacation with you.

Yard Stick

To see or use a yard stick in your dream, denotes that your exacting ways are disliked by others and because of this, you are often ignored.

Yarn

To dream that you are working with yarn and experience difficulty in undoing it, predicts slight irritation due to disappointments. To handle it successfully, success in whatever you may attempt. For a young woman to dream of yarn, denotes that her lover greatly respects her.

Yawning

To dream of seeing others yawn, means unpleasant conditions and even illness to the dreamer. To yawn yourself, denotes that you are restless, nervous, and never satisfied with your life.

Yell

To emit a yell in your dream, means that you will be discovered in an unworthy plot. To hear the yell of another, is a sign that you will be of help to an old friend in the near future.

Yoke

To dream of wearing a yoke of any kind, is a sign that you will do hard labor under an exacting taskmaster. To dream of seeing a yoke of oxen, foretells a new address quite distant from your present place of abode.

Youth

For an elderly person to dream of his or her youth, denotes continuing ease and comfort.

Z

"Therefore night shall be unto you, that ye shall
not have a vision, and it shall be dark unto you,
that ye shall not divine; and the sun shall go
down over the prophets, and the day shall be dark
over them."

Michah iii, 6

Zebra

To dream of seeing a herd of zebras, denotes that you are wasting time and energy on something that will prove harmful to you. To dream you see one that is tame, or that you pet one, denotes profits from a source that will delight you and result in much joy.

Zephyr

To dream of soft zephyrs, relates to sentiment. You will sacrifice a great deal for the one you love and let sentiment interfere with business. For an unmarried woman to dream that she is depressed by zephyrs, denotes petty uneasiness and restlessness.

Zipper

To dream of fastening one's clothes with a zipper, is a sign that you will preserve your dignity in the face of provocation to do otherwise. If you dream of a zipper getting stuck, you will be chagrined by the actions of one of your friends.

Zinc

To dream of zinc, omens good luck to the dreamer. Business will soon climb to a paying basis, resulting in an increase in cash-flow. The dreamer may enjoy many benefits and luxuries due to this extra income.

Zodiac

To dream of seeing or studying the system of the zodiacs, predicts fame and riches to the dreamer through his love for wisdom and charity.

Zoo

To dream of looking at animals in a zoo, foretells that you will travel to far-off places. To dream of taking a child to a zoo, you will make a great deal of money.